ETHNIC CHRONOLOGY SERIES
NUMBER 3

The Jews in America
1621-1970
A Chronology & Fact Book

Compiled and edited by
Irving J. Sloan

1971
OCEANA PUBLICATIONS, INC
DOBBS FERRY, NEW YORK

DEDICATION

To Michael and Helen Rhodes
whose commitment to knowledge
of the Jews is what keeps Jewish
life everlasting .

––––––––––

Library of Congress Cataloging in Publication Data

Sloan, Irving J   comp.
    The Jews in America, 1621-1970.
    (Ethnic chronology series)
    CONTENTS: The Jews in America; a chronology.
--Selected documents of American Jewry. -- Appendices:
Estimated American Jewish population by State. Selected
and annotated bibliography (p.   ) [etc.]
    1.   Jews in the United States--History--Chronology.
2.   Jews in the United States--History--Sources.
3.   Jews in the United States--Bibliography. I.   Title.
II.   Series.
E 184.J5S57   973'.04'924   72-170976
ISBN   0-379-00500-X

Manufactured in the United States of America

E
184
.J5
S57

Sloan, Irving J., comp.
    The Jews in America, 1621-1970: a chronology & fact
book. Compiled and edited by Irving J. Sloan. Dobbs
Ferry, N.Y., Oceana Publications. 1971.
        v. 151 p. 23 cm.
    Ethnic chronology series no. 3
    Includes bibliographical references.
    The Jews in America: a chronology.—Selected
documents of American Jewry.—Appendices: Estimated
American Jewish population by State. Selected and
annotated bibliography (p. 122-124) Audio-visual
materials on American Jewish life and history (p.
125-128) American Jewish civic organizations. American

(CONTINUED ON NEXT CARD)

EDITOR'S FOREWORD

Cultural and racial pluralism have become increasingly the dominant theme in American life and history. The diversity of origins among the peoples of the United States is viewed as a national asset and strength. This is as it should be. "From Many--One" remains an appropriate expression. The "oneness" of the many which make up the American nation is the commitment of all to the democratic principles by which all Americans live. Among those principles is the respect every group owes to the other in their pursuit of life, liberty, and happiness.

This small volume seeks to bring together in a summary way the people and events in American Jewish history which can provide the reader with at least an outline of the particular contribution of the American Jews to American civilization. Eventually, a series of similar volumes will relate the distinctive role each of America's racial and ethnic groups have played to make the nation what it is today.

But turning to the subject of this particular Chronology and Fact Book, the American Jew, no one can fail to be impressed if not amazed at the scope of the achievements of this relatively small minority group. At least one unique aspect of the activity of the American Jew is the great willingless and dedication he showed and continues to show not only to his fellow Jews both within and without the nation, but the assistance in terms of talent and funds to fellow Americans of every ethnic and racial persuasion. Especially do the documents reveal this about the American Jew.

The author proudly states that he is an American Jew, and in researching and preparing this work he takes great pride in what he learned about his fellow-Jews in America. Hopefully, students and readers will share this pride because the achievement of America owes no small measure of that achievement to the Jew in American life and history. By the same token, the American Jew must acknowledge and appreciate the opportunity the peoples of this nation have provided for all to make these contributions which together are what makes the nation what it is, in Whitman's words, "a nation of nations."

THE JEWS IN AMERICA
A CHRONOLOGY

CHRONOLOGY

1621   Elias Legardo came to Virginia on the <u>Abigail</u>, the first Jew to arrive in this colony.

1649   Solomon Franco was recorded as the first Jew in the colony of Massachusetts when he was ordered to return to Holland.

1654   Jacob Barsimon arrived in New Amsterdam from Holland on the ship, <u>Peartree</u>. He was the first Jewish settler in what is now New York City.

Twenty-three Jews arrived in New Amsterdam on board the <u>St. Charles</u>, from Recife, Brazil.

1655   Jacob Barsimon and Asser Levy petitioned New Amsterdam's Governor Peter Stuyvesant "to be permitted to keep the guard with other burghers, or be free from tax."

A resolution of the Governor and Council of New Amsterdam exempted Jews from military service of standing guard, and imposed instead a special tax on them.

The Dutch West India Company issued an order decreeing that the Jews had a right to remain in New Amsterdam over the objections of Governor Stuyvesant.

New Amsterdam Jews won the right to trade and travel along the Hudson and Delaware Rivers.

1656   Jews were permitted to establish a Jewish burial ground in New Amsterdam.

Jews could own their own homes in New Amsterdam.

Jacob Lumbrozo was the first known Jew in Maryland upon his arrival in this year. He was one of the first medical doctors to practice in the colonies.

1657   Asser Levy was admitted to the right of burgher, paving the way for citizenship rights for other Jews and minority groups in the colony of New Amsterdam.

1660   Asser Levy was initiated as the first kosher butcher on the American continent. His shop was located on Wall Street in New Amsterdam.

1662   The first group of Jews settled in Newport, Rhode Island.

1671   Money for building the first Lutheran church in New York City was made available through a loan from Asser Levy.

1672   The Council for Plantations in England decreed in the case of Rabba Couty, a New York Jew, that Jewish freemen on British soil were not aliens.

1674   Jews gained full religious liberty under appointment of Edmund Andros as Governor of New York colony.

1681   Asser Levy died.

1682   Jews rented a house on Beaver Street in New York City for their first synagogue, Congregation <u>Shearith Israel</u> (Remnant of Israel).

1684   The General Assembly of Rhode Island ruled that Jews may live and do business despite the fact that they were "strangers" in the colony.

1688   Abraham Campenelli became the first Jewish freeman in Rhode Island.

1703   Luis Gomez, one of the major merchants of the colonial period, settled in New York City.

1705   Jews introduced soap-making in Rhode Island.

1720   David Franks, leading merchant in Philadelphia before the Revolution and devoted Tory, was born in New York City.

              Judah Monis was the first Jew in America to have a college degree and the first Jewish graduate of Harvard College. Although he was later converted to Christianity by Increase Mather two years later, he served for 40 years as Hebrew instructor at Harvard.

1723   Myer Myers, a silversmith and the first native born artist of English America, was born in New York City.

1728   The Jews of New York City received official permission to build a synagogue.

1733   The first group of Jews to settle in Georgia arrived from England.

1735   Mordecai Sheftall, who played an important part
in the Revolutionary War in Georgia, was born in
Savannah.

Joseph Simon, one of the founders of Louisville,
Kentucky, first arrived in this country.

The first Hebrew grammar textbook in America was
published by Judah Monis.

1738   Nathan Levy bought the first Jewish cemetery in
Philadelphia.

1740   The British Parliament passed a law enabling Jews
in the colonies to become naturalized citizens
after 7 years of residence.

Haym Solomon, who was to become a major figure
in the American Revolution, was born in Lisa,
Poland.

1745   Gershom Mendez Seixas, the first rabbi of Congregation Shearith Israel, America's first synagogue,
was born in New York City.

1748   Jacob Rodriguez Rivera, who introduced the sperm
oil industry and the manufacture of spermoceti
candles in America, settled in Newport, Rhode
Island.

1752   Aaron Lopez, the "merchant prince of New England,"
arrived in Newport, Rhode Island, from Lisbon,
Portugal.

1762   Judah Monis died.

1765   Nine Jews were among the 375 merchants who
signed the Non-Importation Agreement of Philadelphia, protesting the "Restrictions, Prohibitions
and ill-advised Regulations" imposed upon the
colonies by British mercantile policy.

1774   Francis Salvador, an English Jew of Portuguese
ancestry, was elected to the General Assembly
of South Carolina.

1775   Judah Touro, philanthropist who acquired a fortune
which was distributed at his death to causes in
America and Jerusalem, was born in Newport, Rhode
Island.

1776   There were about 2000 Jews in America at the out-set of the Revolution.

Francis Salvador of Charleston, South Carolina, was the first Jew to die in the American Revolutionary War.

1777   Mordecai Sheftall was given the rank of Colonel and became Commissary General of Purchases and Issues to the Militia of Georgia.

1778   Moses Levy was admitted to the Pennsylvania Bar and was America's first Jewish lawyer.

1781   Rebecca Gratz, the model for Scott's "Rebecca" in Ivanhoe, was born in Philadelphia. She started the first Jewish Sunday School in America.

1785   Haym Solomon, honored by the nation for his contribution to the winning of the Revolution through his financial genius, died.

1786   Myer Myers was elected president of the Silver-smiths of New York, thus becoming the country's first Jewish member of a trade guild.

Aaron Levy founded the Town of Aaronsburg, Pennsylvania.

1787   Jonas Phillips submitted a proposal for religious equality to the Constitutional Convention in Philadelphia.

1790   George Washington sent his famous letter to the Jewish Congregation of Newport after visiting that city in Rhode Island. He endorsed the spirit of tolerance in the United States in this message.

Hayman Levy, furrier and Indian trader who employed John J. Astor, died.

1791   Benjamin Gomez was listed in New York's directory as a bookseller at 32 Maiden Lane. He was the new nation's first Jewish bookseller.

Ephraim Hart, with 21 others, organized the first Board of Brokers which later became the New York Stock Exchange. Hart later became a partner of John J. Astor.

1793   Isaac Frank was host to President George Washington on his estate in Germantown, Pennsylvania, where Washington went to escape an epidemic of yellow fever in the national capital, Philadelphia.

1796   Dr. Isaac Jacobi invented the laryngoscope and was viewed as the "father of pediatrics."

1799   Levi Myers served as the Apothecary-General of South Carolina.

1801   David Emanuel became Governor of Georgia. His Jewish ancestry has been confirmed by the curator of the American Jewish Historical Society after many years of controversy.

1802   Judah Touro migrated from Newport to New Orleans where he founded the Jewish community and himself grew wealthy as a merchant. His philanthropic activities benefited Jews and non-Jews.

1804   Moses Sheftal was one of the incorporators of the Georgia Medical Society.

1805   The first Jewish writer in the United States, the drama critic of Charleston, South Carolina, Isaac Harby wrote a neo-classic drama, <u>Alexander Severus</u>.

1806   Dr. Joel Hart was recorded as a founder of the New York Medical Society.

1809   Jacob Henry of North Carolina was elected to the state legislature, and won a challenge to be seated on the ground that he was a Jew.

          Rabbi David Einhorn, the intellectual leader of Reform Judaism in the United States, was born.

1811   Judah P. Benjamin, the Jewish spokesman for the Confederacy, was born in the Virgin Islands.

1812   The first copper rolling mill in the United States was built by Harmon Hendricks at Soho, New Jersey. The firm of Hendricks Brothers is the 2nd oldest firm in the country.

          Captain Uriah P. Levy, a hero in the War of 1812, was instrumental in having flogging in the United States Navy abolished this year.

1812   Captain Mordecai Myers of New York led a victor-
        ious charge against the British during the War of
        1812 at Chrysler's Farm near Williamsburg, Virgin-
        ia.

1813   Mordecai Noah was appointed by President James
        Madison as American Consul to Tunis, making him
        the first Jew in the United States to hold a high
        diplomatic post in the Foreign Service.

1817   Joseph Jonas, born in England, arrived in Cincin-
        nati, Ohio, as the first Jew to settle in that area.

1820   Moses Elias Levy founded a settlement in Alachus
        County, Florida, while Florida was still under
        Spanish rule.

        Mordecai Noah petitioned the State of New York
        for a grant of land to establish a Jewish colony in
        the United States.

1822   Mordecai Noah was elected High Sheriff of New
        York.

1823   Solomon Jackson founded the Jew, the first Jewish
        newspaper in the United States devoted exclusive-
        ly to Jewish affairs.

1824   A group of dissidents in Congregation Beth Elohim
        in Charleston, South Carolina, petitioned the
        trustees to introduce certain innovations in the
        service. This was the first organized effort for
        reform which later led to the Reform Judaism move-
        ment in the United States.

        The Jewish community of Cincinnati, Ohio, was
        established.

1825   B'nai Jeshrum was founded as the second congreg-
        ation in the United States. It was located in New
        York City.

1826   The Maryland legislature passed an amendment to
        its Constitution which would permit persons
        "professing the Jewish religion" to hold public
        office and to practice law.

        Dr. Daniel Peixotto, pioneer in the field of vacci-
        nation, won the New York Medical Society Prize
        for his paper on the whooping cough.

| 1832 | The Jewish community of Louisville, Kentucky, was established. |
| | |

1832   The Jewish community of Louisville, Kentucky, was established.

1833   Uriah P. Levy purchased Jefferson's homestead, Monticello, later passing it on as a public Jefferson memorial.

1837   The Jewish community of Chicago, Illinois, was established.

1839   The Jewish communities of St. Louis, Missouri, and Cleveland, Ohio, were established.

1840   Dr. Charles H. Lieberman successfully performed the first operation of strobismus in the United States.

1842   Adam Gimbel opened the first American department store, a small shop in Vincennes, Indiana.

Alexander Kohurt, one of the founders of Conservative Judaism in the United States, was born in Hungary.

1843   B'nai B'rith was organized in New York as the first Jewish fraternal organization in the world.

Ohabei Shalom synagogue was organized by German immigrants. Its Orthodox house of worship was the first built in Boston.

1847   Jacob Henry Schiff, one of the leading American-Jewish philanthropists, was born in Frankfurt, Germany. He came to the United States in 1865.

1849   Rabbi Morris Jacob Raphall came to Congregation B'nai Jeshrum in New York City. He was the spokesman for the small pro-slavery faction among American Jewry.

Emma Lazarus, the poetess who wrote "The New Colossus" which is inscribed on a plaque imbedded in the Statute of Liberty, was born in New York City.

1850   Samuel Gompers, the great labor leader who was a founder of the American Federation of Labor, was born in England of Dutch-Jewish parents.

1852   Beth Hamidrash was established as the first Russian-Jewish congregation in the United States.

1853   Judah P. Benjamin was elected to the United States
        Senate as a Whig. He later served the Confederacy
        as Attorney-General, Secretary of War, and Secre-
        tary of State.

        Solomon Nunes Carvalho joined John C. Fremont's
        expedition to explore the Far West. Carvalho made
        the map, which routes followed over the Rockies
        into California. He was also a leading portrait
        painter.

1854   The first Reform Congregation in the United States
        was founded by Rabbi Isaac M. Wise in Cincinnati.

        Dr. Abraham Jacobi invented the laryngoscope. He
        was also regarded as the "father of the pediatric
        profession."

        American Jews petitioned the United States Senate
        to refuse to ratify a treaty with Switzerland because
        the Swiss Confederation denied certain rights and
        privileges to American Jews who might travel there.

        The first Young Men's Hebrew Association (YMHA)
        was opened in Baltimore, Maryland.

1855   Rabbi David Einhorn came from Austria to serve
        Baltimore's Har Sinai Congregation. He later be-
        gan an abolitionist crusade in pro-slavery Mary-
        land.

1856   Louis Marshall, leading civil libertarian lawyer
        and statesman, was born in Syracuse, New York.

        Louis D. Brandeis, Supreme Court Justice and
        Zionist leader, was born in Louisville, Kentucky.

1858   Adolph S. Ochs, publisher of the N.Y. Times, was
        born in Cincinnati, Ohio.

        Dr. Mary Anna Elson was the first Jewish woman
        to graduate from Pennsylvania Women's Medical
        College.

        Marcus M. Marks, a founder of Educational
        Alliance Settlement House, and originator of the
        "daylight saving time" movement, was born.

        Samuel Untermyer, leading lawyer and organizer
        of the Bethlehem Steel Corporation, was born in
        Lynchburg, Virginia.

1859   Moritz Pinner, a Missouri abolitionist, published the first issue of the Kansas Post.

Rabbi Samuel Meyer Isaacs organized the Board of Delegates of American Israelites, the first body representing a sizable segment of American Jewry to defend Jewish rights.

1860   A rabbi opened a session of Congress with prayer for the first time, recognizing the equal status of Judaism with Christianity.

Abraham Cahan, novelist and editor of the Jewish Daily Forward, was born.

Henrietta Szold, founder of Hadassah, was born in Baltimore, Maryland.

1861   Daniel De Leon organized the medical department of the Confederacy and was the first Surgeon-General of the Confederacy.

Rabbi David Einhorn was forced to flee Baltimore because of the anti-slavery views he expressed on his pulpit at Har Sinai Temple.

1862   Jacob Frankel became the first American rabbi appointed to the Chaplaincy Corps of the United States Army.

General U.S. Grant issued General Order No. 11, an anti-Semitic edict barring Jews from the Tennessee Department of the Army.

Julius Rosenwald, president of Sears, Roebuck & Company from 1910-1925, and noted philanthropist to both Jewish and Black organizations, was born in Springfield, Illinois.

1863   Abraham Lincoln revoked General Grant's General Order No. 11.

1864   Sgt. Leopold Kapeles was the first American Jew to receive the Congressional Medal of Honor.

At the end of the Civil War there were 9 Jewish generals, 18 colonels, 9 lieutenant-colonels, 40 majors, 205 captains, 325 lieutenants, 48 adjutants, and 25 surgeons, in the Union Army.

Dr. David Camden De Leon, a Jewish doctor in Charleston, South Carolina, opened the first drug store in the United States.

1865   Dr. Jonathan P. Horowitz was Chief of the Bureau
        of Medicine and Surgery in the United States Navy.
        He projected and constructed the Naval Hospital in
        Philadelphia.

1866   Abraham Flexner was born in Louisville, Kentucky.
        His studies in American education, especially
        Medical Education in the United States and Canada,
        were landmarks in the history of American medical
        education.

        The Jewish Hospital in Philadelphia was founded.

1867   Lillian D. Wald, one of the great social work pion-
        eers in the United States, was born in Cincinnati,
        Ohio.

        Isaac Lesser opened Maimonides College in Phila-
        delphia, one of the earliest institutions for rabbin-
        ate and other higher Hebrew learning.

1870   Joseph B. Strauss, designer of the direct lift bridge
        and the construction of the Golden Gate Bridge in
        San Francisco, was born in Cincinnati, Ohio.

1871   Felix Warburg, one of the founders of the Hebrew
        University and the Jewish Agency, was born in
        Hamburg, Germany. He was also one of the great
        philanthropist-financiers in the United States.

1872   Isaac W. Bernheim organized the Bernheim Distill-
        ing Company in Louisville, Kentucky. It became
        one of the largest in the United States and is now
        an important unit of Scheneley Distillers.

1873   Leopold Damrosch, a Prussian Jew, became the
        first Jewish orchestra conductor in the United
        States when he was appointed the first conductor
        of the New York Philharmonic Orchestra.

1874   Arnold Schonberg, composer of modern music, was
        born.

        Stephen S. Wise, rabbi, author, and Zionist leader,
        was born in Budapest, Hungary.

        David Lubin opened the first store in the United
        states selling merchandise at retail with fixed
        prices marked on each item. He also established
        the first mail order house in the country.

1875   The Union of American Hebrew Congregations was
         founded by Rabbi Isaac M. Wise.

         Hebrew Union College, the oldest rabbinical
         school in the United States, was founded by
         Rabbi Isaac M. Wise in Cincinnatti, Ohio. This
         has become the theological center for Reform Judaism.

         Fritz Kreisler, violinist and composer, was born in
         Vienna, Austria.

1876   Sophie Irene Loeb, social worker who brought
         about many social reforms in the United States,
         was born in Russia. She was responsible for the
         first Mother's Pension Act in New York State in
         1915 and the penny lunch system in New York City
         public schools.

1877   Emile Berliner made the Bell telephone possible by
         inventing a microphone which was used as a tele-
         phone receiver. This invention also made radio
         broadcasting possible.

         Harry Houdini, one of the world's greatest magici-
         ans, was born in Wisconsin. He was the son of a
         rabbi.

         The first open case of anti-Semitism in the United
         States since Grant's notorious General Order No. 11
         was the refusal of the largest hotel in Saratoga,
         New York, to admit Jewish guests.

         The first free kindergarten in the United States was
         established by Felix Adler.

1878   The Board of Delegates of American Israelites
         surrendered its functions to the Union of American
         Hebrew Congregations, and its name was changed
         to Board of Delegates of Civil and Religious Rights.

1880   Morris R. Cohen, one of the nation's leading philo-
         sophers and regarded as one of the greatest teach-
         ers of his time at the City College of New York, was
         born in Russia.

         There were about 230,000 Jews in the United States.

         Jacob Epstein, called the world's greatest portrait
         sculptor, was born in New York City.

1881   Max Weber, one of the nation's most vigorous
         artists, was born in Russia.

1881   Irving Berlin, who wrote over 700 songs many of
        which have been the most popular melodies in the
        country, was born in Russia.

        Adolpheus S. Solomon founded the American Red
        Cross in Washington, D.C.

1882   The Yiddish theatre in America was established by
        Abraham Goldfaden in New York City.

        Samuel Gompers succeeded in his efforts to get
        Congress to make the first Monday in September
        a legal holiday to honor the working man.

1884   Carl Koller was the first doctor ever to have used
        cocaine as a local anaesthetic in his specialty,
        eye surgery.

        The Montefiore Hospital for Chronic Diseases was
        founded.

        The early American sculptor, Moses Jacob Ezekiel,
        was born in Richmond, Virginia.

1885   Jerome Kern, composer of Show Boat and many other
        light operas and music for the theatre, was born in
        New York City.

1886   Samuel Gompers was elected the first President of
        the American Federation of Labor.

        David B. Steinman, designer of the George Wash-
        ington Bridge, the Triborough Bridge as well as at
        least a half dozen other important bridges, was
        born in New York City.

1887   Dr. Bernard Sachs discovered the disease of child-
        ren known as Tay-Sachs Disease. He was the auth-
        or of the first American treatise on the nervous dis-
        orders of childhood.

        Dr. Willy Myer introduced cystoscopy and also
        developed new techniques in surgery.

        Barney Balaban, one of the pioneers in the motion
        picture industry and owner of the largest movie
        chain in the United States, was born in Chicago,
        Illinois.

1888   Dr. Simon Baruch was the first to operate success-
        fully on appendicitis   which until then was treated
        medically.

1889   Jacques Loeb of the Rockefeller Institute advanced
            his theory of "tropisms," that all life is condition-
            ed by physical and chemical processes.

            The Semitic Museum, operated by Harvard Univer-
            sity, was established as the nation's first Jewish
            museum.

            Oscar Hammerstein built the Harlem Theatre,
            where he introduced the first operas sung in Eng-
            lish in the United States.

1890   Dr. Joseph Ransohoff of Cincinnati was the first
            American to perform operations on the gall bladder.

            Nathan Straus established a system of sterilization
            and distribution of milk for the poor in New York
            City.

            The first publication of the Jewish Publication
            Society of America, Outline of Jewish History,
            appeared.

1891   Henry Morganthau, Jr., statesman and agricultural
            expert, was born in New York.

            Jacques Lipschitz, the eminent sculptor, was born
            in Lithuania, coming to this country during World
            War II.

1892   Laurence A. Steinhardt, who served as Ambassador
            to Russia, Czechoslovakia, Canada, Sweden, and
            Peru, was born.

1894   Andrew Freedman, founder of Maryland Fidelity &
            Guarantee Company of North America Insurance
            Companies, purchased the New York Giants base-
            ball club.

            Dr. Simon Flexner first recorded anaphylaxis. He
            organized the Rockefeller Institute of Medical
            Research in 1903 and served as its Director until
            1945.

            Benjamin V. Cohen, leading New Deal advisor to
            President Franklin D. Roosevelt, was born in
            Muncie, Indiana.

1895   Dr. Albert Ashton Berg performed the first operat-
            ion for volvulus of the stomach.

1895   Maurice Samuel, author and lecturer, was born in Rumania, coming to this country in 1914.

1896   Isador and Nathan Straus took on sole ownership of R.H. Macy, which was to become the largest department store in the world.

Richard Goltheil, orientalist scholar, Professor of Semitic languages at Columbia University, founder and first President of the Zionist movement in the United States, was appointed head of the Oriental Department of the New York Public Library. He served in this position until his death in 1936.

The Jewish Agricultural & Industrial Aid Society was incorporated in New York. It was established by joint action of the Jewish Colonization Society and the Baron de Hirsch Fund.

1897   Abraham Cahan became editor of the Jewish Daily Forward.

Walter Winchell, the most influential newspaper and radio commentator of his time, was born in New York City.

1898   Israel Zangwell delivered his first lecture in the United States.

Isiah Temple in Chicago was dedicated.

1900   Rabbi Isaac Mayer Wise died at age 81.

Aaron Copland, one of the great contemporary composers, was born in Brooklyn, New York.

The International Ladies Garment Workers Union was founded.

The first national labor fraternal organization, the Workmen's Circle, was organized.

1901   Jascha Heifetz, the great violinist, was born in Russia.

The American Smelting & Refining Company came under the control of Meyer Guggenheim and his sons. The Guggenheim family has become one of the leading philanthropists in the nation.

1902   Oscar S. Straus was appointed a member of the Permanent Court of Arbitration at the Hague.

1903   The Jewish Advocate, the largest and the most
            influential Anglo-American newspaper in the
            United States, was established in Boston.

            Solomon Schecter was elected President of the
            Jewish Theological Seminary of America.

1904   Vladimir Horowitz, the eminent concert pianist,
            was born in Kiev, Russia.

            J. Robert Oppenheimer, leading nuclear physicist
            who played a major role in the development of the
            atomic bomb, was born in New York City.

1905   One hundred and twenty-five thousand Jewish
            workers demonstrated against Russian atrocities
            committed against Jews in Russia. The demonstrat-
            ion took place in Union Square in New York City.

            The United States Congress passed a Joint Resol-
            ution expressing sympathy with the Jewish victims
            of Russian massacres raging in that country.

1906   James Loeb established the American Institute of
            Musical Art.

            Adolph J. Sabath was elected to Congress from the
            50th Illinois District and subsequently served the
            greatest number of consecutive terms of any member
            of Congress in his time-- 21 terms.

            Oscar S. Straus was the first Jew to hold a Presid-
            ential cabinet position when President Theodore
            Roosevelt appointed him as Secretary of Commerce.

            Artur Rubinstein, the distinguished pianist, came
            to the United States for the first time.

1907   Simon Guggenheim was elected United States
            Senator from Colorado, He served until 1913.

            Albert A. Michelson received the Nobel Prize in
            Physics for developing optical measuring instrum-
            ents.

1908   Irving Lehman was designated Chief Justice of the
            highest court in New York State, the Court of
            Appeals.

            The Jewish Community of New York City (Kahillah)
            was organized.

1908   Cyrus Adler was named Associate of the Smithson-
            ian Institution in Washington, D.C.

            Leo Rosten, creator of Hyman Kaplan*** and a
            leading social scientist, was born in Poland.

            Arthur J. Goldberg, jurist and statesman, was born
            in Chicago.

            The United Hebrew Charities of New York City
            ceased to be the principal factor in work at Ellis
            Island caring for Jewish immigrants. From this time
            on the work would be directed by the Jewish Imm-
            igration Committee, composed of representatives
            of societies dealing with the Jewish immigrant.

1909   The first coin bearing the head of a President of
            the United States, the Lincoln penny, issued by
            the Treasury Department, was designed by the
            Jewish artist, Victor David Brenner.

            Lillian Wald was appointed member of the New
            York Immigration Commission.

1910   Dr. Isador H. Coriat published Abnormal Psychology,
            the first treatment of this subject in the United
            States.

            Yonah Shimmel developed the Americanized version
            of the East European kasha and potato knishe.

            The Episcopal Convention held in Cincinnati, Ohio,
            voted to discontinue missionary propaganda among
            Jews in the United States.

1911   The American Jewish Committee was incorporated
            by Act of the New York legislature.

            Public School # 9 of New York City opened a kosher
            kitchen for 2000 pupils, furnishing meals at 3¢
            each.

            Associated Press dispatches from St. Petersburg,
            Russia, gave circumstantial accounts of the
            alleged murder by Jews of Christian boys for
            "ritual" purposes.

            The Triangle Waist Company fire in New York City
            killed 143 women, mostly Jewish. This tragedy
            brought about strong legislation dealing with work-
            ing conditions in the city.

1912 The "scratch" method in the study of allergy was initiated by Dr. O. M. Schloss.

Casimir Funk originated the word _vitamin_.

A state organization was formed in Boston to encourage the naturalization of Jews in Massachusetts.

The Philadelphia _Kehillah_ requested leniency in the enforcement of the drastic Sunday law of 1794. The Mayor promised due consideration to those who observed Saturday as their Sabbath.

The Grand Officers of Independent Order Brith Abraham granted the sum of $1000 to families of Jewish strikers in Lawrence, Massachusetts, and appealed to all lodges in support.

Jewish community of Philadelphia called on managers of theatres to protest caricaturing of Jew on the stage.

1913 At Roxbury, Massachusetts, Jews at mass meeting adopt resolution protesting assaults upon them and demanding more adequate protection.

Henry Morganthau was appointed Ambassador to Turkey by President Woodrow Wilson.

Samuel Goldwyn, the first motion picture producer in the United States, released _The Squaw Man_, the first full length film made in Hollywood.

The Massachusetts Society for Prevention of Cruelty to Animals issued a pamphlet urging nation-wide crusade for abolition of _shechitah._

At Passaic, New Jersey, High School, 29 members of the Senior Class walked out during Class election, alleging racial discrimination.

Alpha Delta Phi fraternity withdrew its charter from the chapter at City College of New York because the "Hebraic element is greatly in excess, " and the College has therefore lost its potential as a field for the organization.

A mass meeting was held in New York City under the auspices of the Federation of Oriental Jews to consider relief of Jews affected by Balkan War.

1914   The United States Bureau of Immigration instructed
        immigration commissioners to avoid deporting Jews
        on Jewish holidays.

        Der Tag (The Day), a Yiddish newspaper, was
        founded by Herman Bernstein, the journalist,
        novelist, and playwright.

        Sidney Hillman was elected the first President of
        the Amalgamated Clothing Workers, which was to
        become under his leadership a model labor union
        in the American labor movement.

        The Semitic Division of the Library of Congress
        was established with Dr. Israel Shapiro in charge.

        The Anti-Defamation League was founded by the
        Independent Order B'nai B'rith, to eliminate publ-
        ication of literature prejudicial to the reputation
        of Jews.

        Jonas E. Salk, medical researcher and educator,
        developer of the Salk anti-polio vaccine, was born
        in New York City.

1915   Harry Plotz, bacteriologist at Mt. Sinai Hospital
        in New York City, succeeded in isolating typhus
        fever bacillus.

        A stadium was presented by Adolph Lewisohn to
        City College of New York.

        Moses Alexander was the first Jewish governor
        when he was elected as Governor of Idaho. He
        held two terms.

1916   Harvard University refused to change the date of
        examinations scheduled for Yom Kippur, but
        granted permission to Jewish students to dictate
        answers to stenographers.

        Leo M. Frank, leading figure in a celebrated
        murder trial in Atlanta, Georgia, was lynched by
        a mob after his conviction on evidence since
        proved to be false.

        The Jewish agricultural colony in Clarion, Utah,
        was abandoned because of hard times due to poor
        crops.

        Louis D. Brandeis was nominated as the first
        Associate Justice to the United States Supreme

Court who was of the Jewish faith.

Yehudi Menuhin, the child prodigy violinist who
became one of the world's great artists during his
manhood, was born in New York City.

1917   Herbert Bayard Swope won the first Pulitzer Prize
        for newspaper reporting.

        Henry A. Dix, a Russian Jewish immigrant who had
        built up the largest uniform manufacturing business
        in the United States, was invited by the Internatio-
        nal Red Cross to design a nurses' hospital uniform.

        Rabbi Abba Hillel Silver took the pulpit of The
        Temple in Cleveland, Ohio, a post he occupied
        throughout his career as author and Zionist leader.

1918   Leonard Bernstein, composer and conductor, was
        born in Lawrence, Massachusetts.

        Maurice Schwartz founded the Yiddish Art Theatre
        in New York City.

        Belle Moskowitz was Chairman of the Women's
        Division of Alfred E. Smith's first campaign for
        Governor of New York. She served as Smith's
        advisor throughout his career as Governor.

        Alexander Silverman, one of the world's leading
        authorities on the subject of glass and the inventor
        of the illuminator for microscopes, became Chair-
        man of the Department of Chemistry at the Univer-
        sity of Pittsburgh.

        The United States War Department recognized the
        Jewish Welfare Board as the official agency for
        welfare work among Jews in the Army.

        Dr. D.I. Macht, instructor in pharmacology at the
        Johns Hopkins University, announced the discovery
        of a new therapeutic agent, known as bingle
        benzolate, a substitute for medicine derived from
        opium.

1919   The Baltimore Hebrew College and Teachers'
        Training School was opened. It was one of the
        first institutions in the United States to offer a
        full Hebrew teachers' training program.

        Alex Mitchel invented a combination plow and
        tractor.

1919   General John J. Pershing announced that the
        United States War Department was adopting the
        Mogen David to mark graves of Jews who were
        killed in action.

1921   Albert D. Lasker was appointed chairman of the
        United States Shipping Board.

        Golda Meir left Milwaukee, Wisconsin, to
        settle in Palestine with her husband, Morris
        Myerson.

1922   Gerard Swope became president of the General
        Electric Company and served until his retirement
        in 1940.

1923   Lias E. Reiss invented the device for adding
        sound to film which he sold to Lee De Forest.
        He also invented the converter for alternating
        current which made possible the electrification
        of railroads.

1924   Cyrus Adler was elected President of the Jewish
        Theological Seminary of America.

        Serge Koussevitzky became the conductor of the
        Boston Symphony Orchestra, a position he held
        until 1949.

1925   George Gershwin introduced the first jazz piano
        concerto, Concerto in F, in Carnegie Hall.

        Edna Ferber was the first Jewish novelist to win
        the Pulitzer Prize in fiction. The novel was So Big.

        Benny Leonard, who fought 210 bouts and lost 4,
        retired as the undefeated lightweight champion
        boxer and holder of the title for 8 years.

        Rabbi Judah L. Magnes, community leader and
        educator, became President of the Hebrew
        University in Jerusalem.

        Sidney Howard received the Pulitzer Prize for his
        play, They Knew What They Wanted.

1926   Vladimir Horowitz made his American debut as
        soloist with the New York Philharmonic Orchestra.

1927   Al Jolson, one of the most popular entertainers
        in American theatrical history, made the first
        "talking" motion picture, The Jazz Singer.

1927   Henry Ford addressed an apology to the Jews of the
United States for the anti-Semitic campaign he had
been conducting for the past seven years.

Felix Frankfurter, then professor of law at the
Harvard Law School, became a national figure
in liberal political circles as a result of his plea
in defense of the controversial anarchists, Sacco
and Venzetti.

1928   Yeshiva College was dedicated as the first liberal
arts college in the nation which was under Jewish
sponsorship.

Herbert H. Lehman was elected Lieutenant Governor of New York.

Ernest Bloch received the prize for the best symph-
onic work composed by an American, Musical
America.

1929   Elmer Rice won the Pulitzer Prize for his drama,
Street Scene.

Louis Jaffe was awarded the Pulitzer Prize for his
editorial writing in the Norfolk Virginian-Pilot.

Emile Berliner, inventor, scientist, and author,
died.

As a result of widespread Arab uprisings against
Jews in Palestine, the Zionist Organization of
America established a Palestine Emergency Relief
Fund. By the end of the year over $2,000,000 was
contributed to the fund by the American Jewish
community.

A deputation representing the American members of
the Jewish Agency for Palestine was received by
Ramsay MacDonald, Prime Minister of Great Britain,
who was on a visit to the United States. The group
was headed by Felix M. Warburg, who called upon
Great Britain to carry out its Mandate "more symp-
athetically."

The American Jewish Congress called a conference
of national Jewish organizations in New York City
which proclaimed Sunday, March 16, the day set
aside by the Christian churches as the national day
of protest by American Jewry against the persecution
of Jews in Soviet Russia.

1929   The Central Conference of American Rabbis, held
            in Detroit, decided upon a complete revision of
            the Union Prayer Book in use in all Reform Cong-
            regations in the United States.

            The Talmudical Institute of Harlem, as well as
            a number of other Jewish parochial schools, were
            forced to close because of lack of funds resulting
            from the departure of former supporters of the
            schools from the neighborhoods.

            The Young Israel, an orthodox youth agency,
            passed a resolution deprecating the decay of
            the Yiddish language among the Jewish youth, as
            a factor leading to a breach between them and
            their parents.

            The Conference Committee of National Jewish
            Women's Organizations passed a resolution urging
            observance of Jewish dietary laws at all dinners
            and public functions under Jewish auspices, and
            strict adherence to the Sabbath in all public inst-
            itutions maintained by and for the Jewish commun-
            ity.

            The General Committee on Jewish Religious Radio
            Programs, with the cooperation of the National
            Broadcasting Company (NBC), made its facilities
            available for the broadcast of a series of Jewish
            programs over a large network beginning November
            3rd. The aim of the programs would be to foster
            and inspire general human aspirations, and to
            bring out the cultural values of Judaism in their
            relation to the pattern of American life.

            Dr. Julius Maller of Teachers College, Columbia
            University, before the Conference of Religious
            Education Association in Baltimore, reported that
            on the basis of questionnaires answered by child-
            ren in public schools in New York City, 69.6% of
            the boys and 37.2% of the girls received Jewish
            education.

1930   Karl Landsteiner won the Nobel Prize in Physiology
            and Medicine for his discovery of human blood
            groups.

            Eugene Meyer was appointed a Governor of the
            Federal Reserve Board.

            Maxie Rosenbloom held the World Light-Weight

1930   boxing title.

Jerome Frank wrote Law and the Modern Mind,
which introduced the psychological approach to
law.

Herman Bernstein was appointed Minister to
Albania.

Edward E. Brody was appointed Minister to Finland.

Harry F. Guggenheim was appointed Ambassador to
Cuba.

David E. Kaufman was appointed Minister to Siam.

The Council of Jewish Women reported that 10,000
Jewish young women in New York City and 8,000
in Chicago were without employment because of
discrimination. The subject was brought up in the
United States Congress by Congressman Fiorello
H. La Guardia, who charged that such discrimination is practiced against Jews in the appointments
to the U.S. Consular Service. Assemblyman Louis
Lefkowitz of New York City introduced a bill in the
New York State legislature making it a misdemeanor
for an employer to discriminate against an applicant
for work on account of race, creed, or color.

1931   Mortimer J. Schiff was elected president of the
National Council of Boy Scouts of America.

David Belasco, playwright and producer, died in
New York City.

Ben Selling, Oregon's "first citizen," died in
Portland. He served as a member of the state
senate for 8 years, including a term as president.
He was Acting Governor of the state and also
served in the United States House of Representatives where he was Speaker for a short period.

Julius L. Meier was Governor of Oregon.

Frank Boas was elected President of the American
Association for Advancement of Science.

Moses Goodman was elected President of the
American Chemical Society.

Robert D. Kohn of New York was re-elected President of the American Institute of Architects.

1931   Felix M. Warburg was elected President of the
              American Association for Adult Education.

              Daniel Guggenheim, founder of the Guggenheim
              Foundation, died.

              Nathan Straus, founder of Macy's, the world's
              largest department store, died.

              Israel H. Levinthal, President of the Rabbinical
              Assembly of America, urged that the number of
              rabbis graduated by the seminaries and the organ-
              ization of new congregations cease, due to the
              economic depression.

              The President of the Hebrew Union Colleges
              announced that the school was to be discontinued
              because of lack of funds.

              According to figures from the Bureau of Jewish
              Social Research, the number of families receiving
              aid from 30 Jewish agencies in various parts of
              the country was 42.8% greater in 1931 than it was
              in 1930. In Minnesota the increase was reported
              to be 100% greater and in Baltimore the increase
              was 77%.

              The American Palestine Campaign of the Jewish
              Agency for Palestine was inaugurated with a goal
              of raising $2,500,000.

              While several Jewish organizations in the United
              States "were deeply stirred by the results of the
              German elections, they took no action, knowing
              that the sister community in Central Europe is well
              able to deal with the situation, and feeling confi-
              dent that the sober judgment of the mass of the
              German people would not permit German honor to
              be stained by a recrudescence of medieval per-
              secution."

              The Jewish Braille Institute of America was organ-
              ized by the National Federation of Temple Sister-
              hoods and the United Synagogue Council of
              America.

              The publishers of Roget's Thesaurus of English
              Words and Phrases, in which offensive connotat-
              ions of the word "Jew" had been given in all
              editions since it was first published in 1852,
              agreed to eliminate such references.

1931   Rutgers College in New Brunswick, New Jersey,
              authorities admitted that they were limiting the
              number of Jewish admissions "to equalize the
              proportion" and to prevent the University from be-
              coming "denominational. "

1932   Herbert H. Lehman was elected Governor of New
              York.

              George S. Kaufman, Morris Ryskind, and Ira
              Gershwin received the Pulitzer Prize for their
              musical play, Of Thee I Sing. George Gershwin
              wrote the music.

              David Dubinsky began his tenure as president of
              the Ladies' Garment Workers" Union.

              Henry Horner was elected Governor of Illinois.

              The New York Academy of Medicine announced
              that it turned down several bequests and gifts
              because of stipulations such as that "no grants
              should be made to Jews or any other individual
              working in an institution which had a Jew as a
              member of the Board. "

              Benjamin N. Cardozo was appointed by President
              Herbert Hoover as Associate Justice of the United
              States Supreme Court.

              Louis I. Dublin was elected President of the
              American Public Health Association.

              Maurice J. Karpf was elected President of the
              American Association of Schools of Social Work.

              Louis Marcus was elected Mayor of Salt Lake City,
              Utah.

1933   Hank Greenberg joined the Detroit Tigers and
              batted 301. for the start of one of the most import-
              ant baseball careers in American baseball history.

              Albert Einstein came to the United States to be
              associated with the Institute for Advanced Study
              at Princeton, New Jersey.

              A "Statement of Beliefs, " protesting against the
              intolerance against Jewish and other minorities
              in the Hitler Reich, signed by 142 American
              college and university presidents and by 77

1933 outstanding social scientists, was forwarded to
the heads of every institution of higher learning
in Germany by the National Conference of Christian
and Jews.

In response to requests of the Jewish Welfare
Board, the United States government issued orders
granting furloughs to Jews in all the armed services
during the High Holy Days.

Houghton Mifflin Company denied any anti-Jewish
intent in publishing the English translation of
Hitler's Mein Kampf.

The Central Conference of American Rabbis passed
resolutions favoring (1) Recognition of Russia and
(2) Justice for the Negro.

The American Jewish Joint Distribution Committee
announced it raised$1,226,346 for relief of German-
Jewish refugees.

Benjamin Brown, Chairman of the Commission for
Establishment of Jewish Farm Settlements,
announced that 200 Jewish families of unemployed
needle workers will be settled on subsistence
farms in New Jersey and that each family was to
deposit $500 for which it would receive a house,
1 acre of land and necessary farm implements.

It was reported by the Jewish Board of Guardians
that the percentage of Jewish criminals in New
York City had fallen from 14% in 1921 to 7.1% in
1933.

The Zionist Organization of America announced
that since the establishment of the Palestine
Foundation Fund in 1921, a total of $25,000,000
was raised through the Agency.

1934 Barney Ross held three world boxing titles: Light-
weight, Junior Welterweight, and Welterweight.

Henry Morganthau Jr. was appointed Secretary of
Treasury by President Franklin D. Roosevelt.

The Pulitzer Prize for the best drama was awarded
to Sidney Kingsley for Men In White.

1935 The Jewish Daily Bulletin, the only Jewish daily
printed in English, suspended publication.

1935 Mrs. Anna M. Rosenberg was appointed Director
of Region 2 of the Federal Social Security Board.

U.S. Senator William H. King of Utah, urged that
an investigation of Nazi persecution of Jews and
Catholics be made to ascertain if the United States
would be warranted in breaking off diplomatic
relations with Germany.

A crowd of 5000 staged an anti-Nazi demonstration
at the New York City pier where the SS Bremen was
berthed. The Nazi flag was ripped from the staff at
the bow of the ship.

1936 Dr. Otto Loewi received the Nobel Prize in
Medicine for his discovery of the Chemical
transmission of nerve impulses.

The world premier of the English operatic version
of The Dybbuk was held at the Detroit Civic Opera
House.

Dr. Gabriel Davidson, general manager of the
Jewish Agricultural Society, stated in his annual
report that Jewish farmers in the United States
had weathered the economic difficulties of the last
few years and had been making steady progress
in agriculture.

The U.S. House of Representatives unanimously
adopted a resolution authorizing the erection of
a memorial on public grounds for Haym Salomon.

Henry Horner was re-elected Governor of Illinois.

Leon Kroll was awarded the Carnegie International
first prize for his painting, The Road to the Cave.

Herbert H. Lehman was re-elected Governor of
New York.

1937 George Gershwin, the composer, died at the age
of 39 years.

Paul Klapper was appointed President of Queens
College of the City of New York University
system.

William Berman was elected President of the
American Congress of Physical Therapy.

1937   Solomon Blatt was elected Speaker of the South
            Carolina Assembly.

            Charles A. Elsberg was elected president of the
            American Neurological Association.

            Laurence A. Steinhardt was appointed Ambassador
            to Peru.

            Eddie Cantor was elected president of the Ameri-
            can Federation of Radio Artists.

            Walter P. Lewisohn was awarded the Congressio-
            nal Medal of Honor for his part in the Second
            Byrd Antarctic Expedition.

1938   Several times during the year, the activities of
            Nazi sympathizers, in the face of opposition, led
            to rioting and disturbances in many communities
            in the country. One such incident took place at
            a rally conducted by the German-American Bund
            in New York City on the occasion of Adolph Hit-
            ler's birthday. The violence, which erupted when
            American Legionnaires heckled the Nazi speakers,
            resulted in the injury of 7 men and the calling of
            police reserves to protect the meeting.

            At the Second World Conference of the Religious
            Society of Friends held in Swarthmore, Pa., the
            commission on racial justice reported that German
            treatment of the Jews was "a menace to the world."

            Morris R. Cohen was appointed to the faculty of
            the University of Chicago as professor of
            philosophy.

            Herbert H. Lehman was re-elected Governor of
            New York.

            Benjamin N. Cardozo, Associate Justice of the
            United States Supreme Court, died.

            Irving Lehman was re-elected Associate Judge
            of the Court of Appeals of New York State.

            D:, Bela Schick received the Gold Medal of the N.Y.
            Academy of Medicine on the 25th anniversary of the
            publication of his work on immunity in diptheria.

1939 Felix Frankfurter was appointed Associate Justice
of the United States Supreme Court by President
Franklin D. Roosevelt.

Joel E. Spingarn, a founder and president for over
twenty years of the NAACP, died.

Ernest Gruening was appointed Governor of the
Alaska Territory.

The Jewish Agricultural Society noted in its
annual report that 100,000 Jews were settled on
farmlands in the United States.

The Jewish Publication Society of America
announced the appointment of Solomon Grayzel
as editor.

Laurence A. Steinhardt was appointed by President
Franklin D. Roosevelt as Ambassador to Soviet
Russia.

Max Factor, leading cosmetician, died.

1940 Dr. Philip Levine reported a new factor in human
blood now known as the RH factor. He was also
the discoverer of blocking anti-bodies.

The United Jewish Appeal announced that the
increased needs resulting from the war required
a record total of $23,000,000 be raised.

Dr. Cyrus Adler, President of the Jewish Theological Seminary of America and of Dropsie College
for Hebrew and Cognate Learning, died.

Birdie Amsterdam was the first women to be
elected Judge of the Municipal Court of New York
City.

Louis Finkelstein was elected president of the
Jewish Theological Seminary of America.

Irving Lehman was elected Chief Judge of the
New York State Court of Appeals.

Lillian Wald, pioneer social worker, died.

Arthur B. Spingarn was elected president of the
NAACP.

1940   Emma Goldman, internationally known anarchist
            leader, died.

            R.A. Seligman, noted economist and Professor of
            Political Economy at Columbia University, died.

            Samuel Untermyer, leading lawyer and civic leader,
            died.

            Edmund H. Abrahams was appointed Chairman of the
            Advisory Board of the National Park Service.

            Irving Berlin was awarded a placque by the National
            Committee for Music Appreciation for his composi-
            tion, God Bless America.

            Richard C. Neuberger was elected for his first term
            to the State Legislature of Oregon.

            Abraham A. Ribicoff was elected for his first term
            to the State Legislature of Connecticut.

            Charles E. Bloch, "dean of Jewish publishers, "
            died.

            Henry Horner, Governor of Illinois, died.

            Bernard Revel, founder and president of Yeshiva
            College, died.

            Max Steuer, nationally famous criminal lawyer,
            died.

1941   Jan Peerce made his debut at the Metropolitan
            Opera House.

            Associate Justice of the U.S. Supreme Court
            Louis D. Brandeis died.

            Jacob Burck was awarded the Pulitzer Prize for
            the best newspaper cartoon.

            Julius H. Amberg was appointed special assistant
            to the Secretary of War.

            George Blumenthal was re-elected president of the
            Metropolitan Museum of Art.

            Babette Deutsch was awarded the Julia Ellsworth
            Ford Foundation Prize for the best children's book

1941   of the year, <u>Walt Whitman: Builder for America</u>.

Lillian Hellman received the New York Drama
Critics' Circle Award for her drama, <u>Watch on the
Rhine.</u>

Sidney Hillman was appointed Associate Director-
General of the Office for Production Management,
a major war-time federal agency.

Robert Moses received the gold "order of merit"
medal of the National Institute of Arts & Letters
for his "distinguished creative beauty in New York
City."

Simon H. Rifkind was appointed Judge in the
Federal Court for the Southern District of New
York.

Dr. Bela Schick was awarded the Gold Medal of
the Forum for Allergy for his contribution to the
treatment of allergy.

Efrem Zimbalist was appointed Director of the
Curtis Institute for Music in Philadelphia.

1942   The American Jewish Joint Distribution Committee
appropriated $7,250,000 for relief, immigration
aid, educational and reconstructive assistance to
795,000 people abroad during the year.

Senator Scott Lucas of Illinois, speaking at the
annual memorial services of the Jewish War Vet-
erans of the United States in Temple Emanu-El in
New York City, denounced as liars and 5th colum-
nists those who "spread vicious canards that our
Jewish citizens in this war are letting others do
the fighting for them. He pointed out that during
the last war 4% of the men in the United States
armed forces were Jewish. 1,100 of them were
cited for valor, 150 received the Distinguished
Service Cross and 6 of the them received the
Congressional Medal of Honor.

Rabbi Bernard Bergman of New York offered the
invocation in the United States House of Representatives, being the first Orthodox rabbi to
officiate in that capacity.

1945   Aaron Copland was awarded the Pulitzer Prize for
his musical composition, Appalachian Spring.

Joe Rosenthal received the Pulitzer Prize for photography.

Lewis I. Strauss was appointed Rear Admiral in the
United States Navy.

The New York State Board of Regents conferred
university rank upon Yeshiva College, thereby
making Yeshiva the first American university under
Jewish sponsorship.

Bernard M. Baruch was appointed as United States
Representative on the United Nations Atomic
Energy Commission.

Paul M. Herzog was appointed chairman of the
National Labor Relations Board.

Joseph Rosin, chemist, was awarded the American
Pharmaceutical Association Remington Medal, the
highest award of American pharmacy.

Frances Y. Slanger of Boston was the first army
nurse killed in the European theatre of operations
World War II.

Jerome Kern, leading musical composer, died.

Irving Lehman, Chief Judge of the New York State
Court of Appeals, died.

During World War II there were 311 chaplains
serving Jewish servicemen. Of this number, 147
or 47% were Reform; 96 or 31%, were Conservative,
and 68 or 22% were Orthodox.

David Adler, architect, was elected member of the
National Institute of Arts & Letters.

Benjamin V. Cohen was appointed by President
Harry S. Truman as Counsellor of the State Department.

Lillian Hellman, playwright, was elected member
of the National Institute of Arts & Letters.

1945   Herman B. Baruch was appointed Ambassador to
Portugal.

Edwin J. Cohn, professor of biochemistry at Harvard
University, was given the first Passano Foundation
Award of $5000 for his discovery of the elements of
blood plasma valuable in the treatment of surgical
shock.

Joseph Erlanger was awarded, together with Herbert
S. Gasser, the Nobel Prize in Physiology and
Medicine, for their work on the highly differentiated
functions of single nerve fibers.

Sidney Hook received the Butler silver medal of
Columbia University as "graduate who has shown
the most competence in philosophy or education. "

Milton Rosenau was elected president of the
American Public Health Association.

Karl Shapiro won the Pulitzer Prize for his poetry
in <u>V-Letter and Other Poems</u>.

Laurence A. Steinhardt was appointed Ambassador
to the Czechoslovak government-in-exile in
London.

1946   Hermann J. Muller received the Nobel Prize for
Medicine for his discovery of the influence of X-
rays in genetics.

U.S. Senator Jacob V. Javits of New York began
his political career upon his election to the House
of Representatives from the 21st Congressional
District in New York City.

David Lilienthal was appointed as the first chairman of the United States Atomic Energy Commission.

Morris R. Cohen, the philosopher, died.

Irving Berlin was awarded the Medal of Merit, for
service to the USO (United Service Organization)
through his musical production, <u>This Is the Army</u>.

Norman Corwin, radio writer, received the first
Wendell L. Willkie "One World Award. "

Stanley H. Fuld was appointed by Governor Thomas
E. Dewy as Associate Judge of the New York State
Court of Appeals.

1946   Simon Flexner, Director of the Rockefeller Institute
        for Medical Research (forerunner of Rockefeller
        University), died.

        Sidney Hillman, labor leader and presidential ad-
        visor, died.

        Alfred Stieglitz, one of the great photographers in
        the United States, died.

1947   The Touro Synagogue in Newport, Rhode Island, was
        dedicated as a national shrine.

        The Jewish Museum, located in the New York City
        family home of Felix M. Warburg, was opened to
        the public.

        Herman B. Baruch was appointed Ambassador to The
        Netherlands.

        Reports to the Council of Jewish Federations and
        Welfare Funds indicated that its member agencies
        raised more than $160,000,000.

        George W. Armstrong, reputed oil and steel million-
        aire of Fort Worth, Texas, announced that he plan-
        ned to use the Judge Armstrong Foundation (incorp-
        orated for charitable purposes) to promote anti-
        Semitism through the publication of literature aimed
        at arousing feelings against American Jewry.

        Gentleman's Agreement, a frank portrayal of anti-
        Semitism in American life, won the Academy Award
        as the Best Picture of the Year.

        Mrs. Stephen S. Wise, artist and social worker,
        died.

        Compilation of arrivals recorded by the United
        Service for New Americans and by the Hebrew
        Immigrant Aid Society revealed that about 25,885
        Jewish immigrants came to this country during the
        year.

        Ernst Lubitsch, motion picture producer and direc-
        tor, died.

        A total of 31 central bureaus of Jewish education
        reported aggregate budgets of $2,335,000 this
        year.

1948   Brandeis University opened in Waltham, Massachusetts.

Eliahu Elath was named the first diplomatic representative of Israel to the United States.

Nelson Glueck, leading archeologist and biblical
scholar, was designated president of Hebrew
Union College in Cincinnati.

Alan Weyl Bernheimer received the Eli Lilly award
for his outstanding contribution in the field of
bacteriology, presented by the Society of American
Bacteriologists.

Edwin S. Cohn, chairman of the physical chemistry
department at Harvard University Medical School
was awarded the Theodore W. Richards Medal by
the American Chemical Society for his outstanding
work on the physical chemistry of proteins.

The One World Award Committee gave the One
World Award to Albert Einstein.

"Rube" Goldberg received the Pulitzer Prize for
his newspaper cartoon "Peace Today."

The United Jewish Appeal established the largest
fund-raising campaign goal in its history,
$250,000,000.

1949   Former New York Governor Herbert H. Lehman was
elected to the United States Senate. He was the
first Jew to be elected to the Senate by popular
vote.

The Pulitzer Prize for photography was awarded to
Nathaniel Fein of the N.Y. Herald Tribune.

1950   Anna M. Rosenberg was appointed Assistant
Secretary of Defense under George C. Marshall.
She was the first Jewish woman to occupy a high
federal office.

Mrs. Katherine E. White was the first woman in
the United States to be a manager of an American
city when she became city-manager of Red Bank,
New Jersey.

Meyer Berger of the N.Y. Times received the
Pulitzer Prize for General Reporting.

1950   Laurence A. Steinhardt, U.S. diplomat who served
          as Ambassador to 6 countries, died.

          During the period 1900-50 Jewish school enrollment
          grew from 45,000 to 266,609.

          Shmul Cohen, archivist, historian of the Jewish
          labor movement, died.

          Daniel Frisch, major figure in the American Zionist
          movement, died.

          Solomon R. Guggenheim, mining industrialist and
          art patron, died.

          The American Jewish Yearbook reported that
          American Jews were predominantly urban as
          evidenced by the fact that 75% of American Jewry
          lived in communities reporting a Jewish population
          of 40,000 --or more: New York, Washington, D.C.,
          Miami, St. Louis, Los Angeles, Chicago, Phila-
          delphia, Pittsburgh, Cleveland, Newark, Detroit,
          Boston, San Francisco, and Baltimore.

          Max Radin, attorney, educator, author, scholar,
          died.

          Milton Steinberg, rabbi, writer, Zionist leader,
          teacher, leader in Jewish community affairs, rabbi
          of Park Avenue Synagogue in New York City, died.

1951   Eddie Cantor was the first actor in the United
          States to receive an honorary degree, Doctor of
          Humane Letters, Temple University in Philadelphia.

          Albert A. Berg, surgeon, bibliophile, philanthrop-
          ist, pioneer in abdominal surgery, died.

          Fanny Brice, radio and stage star, died.

          Abraham Cahan, editor, author, Socialist and
          labor leader, died.

          Eddy Duchin (Edwin Frank), popular pianist and
          orchestra leader, died.

          The American Jewish Yearbook reported that young
          people between the ages of 15-30 constituted
          22% of the total American Jewish population in
          the United States.

1952   Felix Bloch received the Nobel Prize in Physics
       for developing the nuclear resonance method for
       precision measurements of atomic nuclei magnetic
       fields.

       The Nobel Prize in Medicine was awarded to
       Selman A. Waksman for his work in the discovery
       of streptomycin and its value in treating tuberculo-
       sis.

       Oscar Handlin won the Pulitzer Prize in History
       for his book, The Uprooted.

       The Pulitzer Prize in Fiction was awarded to
       Herman Wouk for The Caine Mutiny.

       Edgar S. Bamberger, executive of the Bamberger
       Department Store, founder and first president of
       station WOR in Newark, New Jersey, died.

       Louis Boudin, labor lawyer and constitutional law
       expert, died.

       Jo Davidson, noted sculptor, died.

       John Garfield, stage and film star, died.

       Arnold Schoenberg, inventor of the controversial
       12-tone (atonal) system in music, died.

       Yeshiva University established a $25,000,000
       building campaign goal for the new medical school
       it scheduled to open in the fall of 1953.

       Over 115,000 Jewish youth belonged to 3500 local
       units of national Jewish youth organizations in the
       United States.

       Sections of Philadelphia were scenes of anti-
       Semitic juvenile incidents during January and
       February of the year. The Miami section of Florida
       had 16 bombings at synagogues and Jewish
       Centers.

       Elihu D. Stone, lawyer and Zionist leader, died.

       Louis Wirth, sociologist, past President of the
       International Sociological Association, American
       Council on Race Relations, and American Sociolog-
       ical Society, died.

1954   Stern College for Women, the first liberal arts
        college for women in the United States under
        Jewish auspices, was opened by Yeshiva University.

        Abraham A. Ribicoff was elected Governor of the
        state of Connecticut.

        The American Jewish Tercentenary was officially
        initiated with a Reconsecration Service at Congreg-
        ation Shearith Israel in New York City, the nation's
        first synagogue, on September 13. For the next
        eight and a half months Jewish religious and secul-
        ar organizations in 250 communities observed the
        Tercentenary with the theme: "Man's opportunities
        and Responsibilities Under Freedom."

        Two previously unpublished centuries-old docum-
        ents, throwing new light on the Jewish struggle for
        civil rights in the New World, were found in the
        Amsterdam Jewish community by Dr. I.S. Emmanuel,
        scholar who had been doing research in Holland.

        A knighthood was awarded to Jacob Epstein, the
        sculptor, who was born on New York's lower East
        Side, by Queen Elizabeth II of England, in her
        semi-annual honors list.

        The 1950 census statistics showed that Jews made
        up 30% of the population of New York City, comp-
        ared to 20% Protestants, and 50% Catholics.

        Rabbi Irving Miller, chairman of the American
        Zionist Council, said "that religious Jews in
        America have every reason to take pride in the role
        they have played in the establishment and the
        building of Israel."

        Louis Broido, chairman of the advisory committee
        of Gimbel Bros. Inc., and active leader in various
        Jewish philanthropic drives, received a plaque as
        Judaism's "Man of the Year" from the Union of
        American Hebrew Congregations and Hebrew
        Union College, the two national institutions of
        Reform Judaism.

        Irving M. Engel was elected president of the
        American Jewish Committee at its annual meeting.

1955   The Albert Einstein College of Medicine, the first
Jewish-sponsored medical school was opened at
Yeshiva University.

The most influential physicist of modern times,
Albert Einstein, died.

A budget of $29,200,000, was adopted by the
American Jewish Joint Distribution Committee at
its 40th anniversary meeting. E. M. Warburg was
re-elected chairman.

An Institute for Ethical Studies in the Atomic Age
was established by the Jewish Theological Seminary
of America.

Rabbi B. Segal reported that Conservative Judaism
membership increased by 150,000 in the past two
years.

The American Jewish Yearbook reported that the
world Jewish population was estimated at 11,867,
000.

United Synagogue of America approved a plan to set
up a division in Israel. All future graduates would
be required to spend one year there as a prerequis-
ite to ordination.

There were 4,257 rabbis in the United States at the
beginning of the year, according to data reported
by the Jewish Statistical Bureau. In 1927 there were
1,751 rabbis, not including those in non-congreg-
ational work.

1956   Hank Greenberg was elected to baseball's Hall of
Fame. He was the first Jew to be so honored.

The Pulitzer Prize for History was awarded to
Richard Hofstadter for his book, The Age of Reform.

Albert Hackett received the Pulitzer Prize for the
play, The Diary of Anne Frank.

The Pulitzer Prize for Fiction was awarded to
MacKinley Kantor for his novel, Andersonville.

The American Jewish Periodical Center was to
microfilm and house Jewish periodicals published
in the United States, 1832-1925; to be established
on the Hebrew Union College campus.

1956   A statement signed by 1,350 rabbis distributed by
            the New York Rabbis Board criticizing the American
            Council for Judaism was issued. It was charged
            that the Council misrepresented the Jewish people,
            maligned the integrity of their institutions, and
            destroyed precepts of Judaism.

            National Council of Churches Yearbook reported
            that 6% of the religious population in the United
            States professed the Jewish faith.

1957   Jerome Frank, educator and jurist, died.

            Max Raisin, rabbi and author, died.

1959   The Nobel Prize in Medicine was received by
            Arthur Kornberg for his contribution to the discovery
            of the pathway for the biosynthesis of DNA.

            Sir Jacob Epstein, the sculptor, died.

            Emilio G. Segre was awarded the Nobel Prize in
            Physics for his discovery of the antiproton.

            Eliot Cohen, editor of Commentary Magazine, died.

            Abraham Flexner, educator and administrator, died.

1960   The only Jewish congregation in Alaska, Beth Sholem
            in Anchorage, affiliated with the Union of American
            Hebrew Congregations.

            Donald A. Glaser received the Nobel Prize in
            Physics for inventing the bubble chamber to study
            subatomic particles.

            Jerry Bock, Sheldon Harnick and Joseph Stein
            received the Pulitzer Prize for their musical play,
            Fiorello!

            The Pulitzer Prize for International Correspondence
            was awarded to A. M. Rosenthal of the N.Y. Times.

            Adele Rosenwald Levy, philanthropist, died.

            Norman Podhoretz was named editor of Commentary,
            one the nation's leading intellectual journals.

            William Maslow was appointed executive director of
            the American Jewish Congress.

1960   A study by the Federation of Jewish Philanthropies
            showed a population figure of 2,114,000 Jews in
            New York City, 27.1% of the total population.

            The Records Center on American Jewish Life was
            established at the Hebrew University in Jerusalem.

            The Yearbook of American Churches reported the
            Jewish population in the United States at 5,500,000.

            Waves of anti-Semitic vandalism hit New York City
            and other areas around the country following similar
            outbreaks in Germany.

1961   William Zuckerman, founder and editor of The Jewish
            Newsletter, died.

            Max Weber, noted artist, died.

            Nathan Straus, business executive and philanthro-
            pist, died.

1962   The Council of Jewish Federations and Welfare Funds
            established a goal of $165,000,000 to meet the local
            and overseas needs for Jewish men, women, and
            children. In its annual report, the Council noted that
            in 1950 about one half of in-patients served by Jew-
            ish hospitals were Jewish. By 1960 this proportion
            had fallen to below 2/5, representing a strengthen-
            ing of nonsecular patterns of service by Jewish hosp-
            itals influenced by changes in population distribution
            and neighborhood composition.

            United Jewish Appeal (UJA) celebrated its 25th
            anniversary since its establishment.

            Brooklyn Hasidic congregation under Rabbi J. Teitel-
            baum bought a 500 acre tract of land in Mt. Olive
            Township, New Jersey, for development of a self-
            contained community.

            An Association of Jewish Book Publishers was estab-
            lished to deal with issues caused by increased sales
            of Jewish text and trade books.

            The Roman Catholic magazine, Commonweal,
            published articles by Rabbi Arthur Herzberg, Daniel
            Danzig and Arthur Cohen on the Jew in American
            society.

            Benjamin Epstein and Arnold Foster of the Anti- Def-

1962   amation League reported that anti-Semitism in the
               United States had sharply declined in the last
               twenty years, but that bias remained a built-in
               part of American life.

               The American Jewish Yearbook reported that the
               United States had the largest Jewish population
               in the world. The Soviet Union ranked 2nd and
               Israel ranked 3rd.

1963   Eugene P. Wigner was a co-winner of the Nobel
               Prize in Physics for his contribution to nuclear and
               theoretical physics.

               Louis Lipsky, Zionist leader, a founder of the
               American Jewish Congress, and writer, died.

               The general non-fiction Pulitzer Prize was awarded
               to Barbara W. Tuchman for her book, The Guns of
               August.

               A record $33,425,000 was raised in six weeks of
               a $39,500,000 emergency fund drive of the United
               Jewish Appeal. The 1964 goal was set at $105,000,
               000.

               The New York City Council of the American Jewish
               Congress formed a special lawyers committee to
               assist black groups in civil rights drive.

               Premier Ben Gurion urged American Jews to develop
               strong cultural ties with Israel.

               World Health Organization (WHO) reported that
               the leukemia incidence was twice as great among
               Jews as among peoples of other faiths.

               A Chair in American Jewish Life was established
               at the Hebrew University in Jerusalem in honor of
               Rabbi Stephen S. Wise.

               Anti-Defamation League Chairman Dore Schary
               deplored anti-Semitism in "new Negro militancy."
               He stressed the Jews' role in the struggle for equal
               rights for all.

               Herbert H. Lehman, former Governor and Senator
               in New York state, died.

               Fritz Reiner, conductor of several of the major
               American symphony orchestras, including the

1963   Chicago and Pittsburgh Symphony Orchestras, died.

            Rabbi Abba Hillel Silver, a leading spokesman for
            American Jewry on many issues, died.

1964   Chaim Gross was elected to membership in the
            National Institute of Arts and Letters in recognition
            of his achievements in art and literature.

            Richard Hofstadter received his second Pulitzer
            Prize in History for his study, Anti-Intellectualism
            in American Life.

            Morris Abram was elected president of the American
            Jewish Committee.

            Malcolm X stated that the experience of Jews in
            achieving participation in American life was a
            lesson for blacks seeking equality.

            The American Jewish Yearbook reported that 80% of
            young Jews attended college in the United States.

            A California University Survey Research Center
            report indicated that 69% of the members of Prot-
            estant congregations questioned believed Jews
            most responsible for the death of Jesus, a factor
            linked to anti-Semitism.

            The Crown Heights, Brooklyn, N.Y., Hasidic
            Jewish community organized a volunteer group,
            "Maccabees of the Community," to patrol areas
            at night in radio-equipped cars to balk attacks
            on Jews.

1965   United States Supreme Court Justice Arthur J.
            Goldberg resigned from the Court to accept the
            appointment as American Ambassador to the
            United Nations.

            Bernard M. Baruch, known as "advisor to Presi-
            dents," died.

            Julian S. Schwinger and Richard P. Feynman were
            recipients of the Physics Nobel Prize for their
            work in quantum electrodynamics.

            Felix Frankfurter, Associate Justice of the United
            States Supreme Court and educator, died.

            Judy Holiday, popular stage and screen actress,
            died.

David Selznick, motion picture producer of a large number of major films, died.

1966 The Pulitzer Prize in History was awarded to Arthur M. Schlesinger, Jr., for his book, A Thousand Days.

Marc Chagall executed two murals for the Metropolitan Opera House in Lincoln Center in New York City.

The Jewish Museum in New York City opened the show, "Lower East Side: Portal to American Life (1870-1924)," which proved to be one of the most popular programs in the institution's history.

The Conference of Presidents of Major American Jewish Organizations voted to become a formal permanent body.

Clergy Concerned About Vietnam urged Jews to spill drops of wine from Sabbath kiddush cups to symbolize shedding of blood in Vietnam.

Harry N. Rivkin was named Dean of Fordham University School of Education, the highest academic post ever given to a Jew there.

Over 500 Conservative and Reform synagogues honored Reconstructionist movement founder Mordecai M. Kaplan on his 85th birthday.

Fordham University appointed a rabbi to the faculty for the first time. He will give courses on Judaism.

Moshe Koussevitsky, popular cantor and concert artist, died.

Sophie Tucker, musical stage star, died.

Max Beer, the well-known journalist, died.

1967 Maurice Samuel received the B'nai B'rith Award for Jewish literature.

The Pulitzer Prize for Fiction was given to Bernard Malamud for his book, The Fixer.

1967   Justin Kaplan received the Pulitzer Prize for his
      biographical work, Mr. Clemens and Mark Twain.

      The Jewish Daily Forward marked its 70th anniver-
      sary as the country's leading Yiddish language
      newspaper.

      The Jewish Theological Seminary of America set up
      an American Jewish Religious Archives to preserve
      original records and other source materials for his-
      tories of Jewish development.

      James Baldwin and Ossie Davis resigned from the
      advisory board of the black nationalist magazine,
      Liberator, to protest series of anti-Semitic
      articles.

      Henry Morganthau, Jr., public servant and
      diplomat, died.

      Bert Lahr, comedy star of radio, stage, and tele-
      vision, died.

      Paul Muni, leading stage and screen actor, died.

      Mischa Elman, violin virtuoso, died,

      Elmer Rice, noted playwright, died.

      Dr. Bela Schick, outstanding medical doctor and
      researcher, died.

1968   Abe Fortas was appointed Chief Justice of the
      United States Supreme Court by President Lyndon
      B. Johnson, but a filibuster against the nomination
      in the Senate forced the President to withdraw the
      nomination.

      Fannie Hurst, the novelist, died.

1969   Marvin Mandel was chosen by the Maryland state
      legislature to replace Vice-President Spiro Agnew
      as Governor of the state.

      The Synagogue Council of America and the
      National Jewish Community Relations Advisory
      Council rejected the reparations demand of the
      National Black Economic Development Conference
      on "both moral and practical grounds."

      Mr. Justice Abe Fortas of the United States

1969   Supreme Court resigned to return to private life
            and law practice.

            Norman Mailer won the Pulitzer Prize for his book,
            The Armies of the Night.

            The Pulitzer Prize for Editorial Writing was awarded
            to Paul Greenberg of the Pine Bluff (Arkansas)
            Commercial.

            Howard Sackler received the Pulitzer Prize for his
            drama, The Great White Hope.

            Ben Shahn, artist-polemicist for liberal political
            causes, died.

            The National Council of Jewish Women marked its
            75th anniversary.

            The American Jewish Committee reported that a
            study of history and social studies text books used
            in junior high and senior high schools in the United
            States contained many errors and misconceptions
            about Jews and a disregard of their achievements.
            Another study, published by the Anti-Defamation
            League, confirmed this conclusion.

            The Council of Jewish Federations and Welfare
            Funds puts the world's Jewish population at
            13,786,000.

            Sister Frances Rhodes spoke to a congregation in
            St. Joseph, Missouri, on tolerance. She is believed
            to be the first nun ever to speak in a synagogue.

            Rabbi A. P. Krause became the first Jewish member
            of the theological faculty at California's Catholic
            University of Santa Clara.

            The Metropolitan Applied Research Center in New
            York City received a $175,000 grant to study
            tensions between blacks and Jews in that city.

1970   Milton J. Shapp was elected Governor of Pennsyl-
            vania.

            The Pulitzer Prize for International Correspondence
            was awarded to Seymour Hersh.

1970   Professor Cyrus H. Gordon of Brandeis University
        maintained that there was evidence that Jews had
        reached America 1000 years before Columbus. He
        cited an inscription found in a Bat Creek, Tenne-
        ssee, burial ground with five letters in the writing
        style of Canaan.

        Dr. William A. Wexler, of the B'nai B'rith Anti-
        Defamation League, was elected chairman of the
        Conference of Presidents of Major American Jewish
        Organizations.

1971   A Hillel Foundation study reported a new type of
        "ethnically conscious and committed" Jewish
        college youth emerging in the United States.

        Two women have registered to take the 5 year
        course at Hebrew Union College of Sacred Music.
        They will be the first women to get professional
        diplomas as cantors.

        A New York Historical Society exhibit marked the
        100th anniversary of laying the cornerstone of
        Central Synagogue in New York City.

        Jewish Student Press reported that 36 Jewish-
        oriented newspapers existed on college campuses
        having a combined circulation of 300,000. New
        ones were coming out at the rate of two a month.

        The United Jewish Appeal opened its 1971 drive
        with an announced goal of $150,000,000.

        The American Jewish Historical Society completed
        documentation of hundreds of manuscripts and data
        dealing with general contributions of Jews and
        Jewish groups to American civilization. Over 3,000,000
        manuscripts and documents and some 50,000 vol-
        umes are housed in the social science research
        center at Brandeis University.

        The Jewish Defense League (JDL), militant Jewish
        organization, joined forces with the Italian-American
        Civil Rights League to fight what both groups called
        harassment by the Federal Government. Rabbi Meir
        Kahane, Director of JDL, contended that his organi-
        zation was rejected by all established Jewish groups.

Dr. M.K. Blaustein gave $1,000,000 to the American
Jewish Committee to establish an institute devoted
to the advancement of human rights.

The third medal in "World's Great Religions" series,
sponsored by Christian Herald Associates, honored
Judaism.

An American Jewish Committee conference charged
that the literary community resents the prominence
of Jews in the arts, particularly in areas of literature,
music, theatre, and films. The Committee also reported
that anti-Zionism has served to legitimize open expression of anti-Semitism.

SELECTED DOCUMENTS
OF
AMERICAN JEWRY

"AS FOREIGN NATIONS CONSENT THAT THE JEWISH NATION MAY GO TO LIVE AND TRADE IN THEIR TERRITORIES"
1655

This is the petition of the some two dozen Jews who arrived in New Amsterdam after fleeing Brazil in 1654 and whose admission was being denied by Governor Peter Stuyvesant. The Dutch West India Company overruled Stuyvesant's objections.

January, 1655

Petition of the Jewish Nation to the Honorable Lords, Directors of the Chartered West India Company, Chamber of the City of Amsterdam.

The merchants of the Portuguese nation residing in this City respectfully remonstrate to Your Honors that it has come to their knowledge that Your Honors raise obstacles to the giving of permits of passports to the Portuguese Jews to travel and to go to reside in New Netherland, which if persisted in will result to the great disadvantage of the Jewish nation. It also can be of no advantage to the general Company but rather damaging.

There are many of the nation who have lost their possessions at Pernambuco and have arrived there in great poverty, and part of them have been dispersed here and there. So that your petitioners had to expend large sums of money for their necessaries of life, and through lack of opportunity all cannot remain here to live. And as they cannot go to Spain or Portugal because of the Inquisition, a great part of the aforesaid people must in time be obliged to depart for other territories of their High Mightinesses the States-General and their Companies, in order there, through their labor and efforts, to be able to exist under the protection of the administrators of your honorable directors, observing and obeying Your Honors' orders and commands.

It is well known to Your Honors that the Jewish nation in Brazil have at all times been faithful and have striven to guard and maintain that place, risking for that purpose their possessions and their blood.

Yonder land is extensive and spacious. The more of loyal people that go to live there, the better it is in regard to the population of the country as in regard to the payment of various excises and taxes which may be imposed there, and in regard to the increase of trade, and also to the importation of all the necessaries that may be sent there.

Your Honors should also consider that the honorable lords, the burgomasters of the city and the honorable high illustrious mighty lords, the States-General, have in political matters always protected and considered the Jewish nation as upon the same footing as all the inhabitants and burghers. Also it is conditioned in the treaty of perpetual peace with the king of Spain that the Jewish nation shall also enjoy the same liberty as all other inhabitants of these lands.

Your Honors should also please consider that many of the Jewish nation are principal shareholders in the Company. They having always striven their best for the Company, and many of their nation have lost immense and great capital in its shares and obligations.

The Company has by a general resolution consented that those who wish to populate the Colony shall enjoy certain districts of land gratis. Why should now certain subjects of this state not be allowed to travel thither and live there? The French consent that the Portuguese Jews may traffic and live in Martinique, Christopher, and others of their territories, whither also some have gone from here, as Your Honors know. The English also consent at the present time that the Portuguese and Jewish nation may go from London and settle at Barbados, whither also some have gone.

As foreign nations consent that the Jewish nation may go to live and trade in their territories, how can Your Honors forbid the same and refuse transportation to this Portuguese nation who reside here and have been settled here well on to about sixty years, many also being born here and confirmed burghers, and this to a land that needs people for its increase?

Therefore the petitioners request, for the reasons given above (as also others which they omit to avoid prolixity), that Your Honors be pleased not to exclude but to grant the Jewish nation passage to and residence in that country; otherwise this would result in a great prejudice to their reputation. Also that by an apostille and act the Jewish nation may be permitted, together with other inhabitants, to travel, live and traffic there, and with them enjoy liberty on condition of contributing like others, etc.

"WHETHER THE JEWISH PEOPLE WHO RESIDE IN THIS CITY SHOULD ALSO TRAIN AND MOUNT GUARD WITH THE CITIZENS' BAND"
1655

The council of New Amsterdam, at the time Peter Stuyvesant was governor, refused the petition of the Jewish residents who sought the right to serve in the militia of the colony. Instead, the council passed the following resolution which subjected the Jews to a special tax.

The captains and officers of the train-bands of this city, having asked the director general and Council whether the Jewish people who reside in this city should also train and mount guard with the citizens' bands, this was taken in consideration and deliberated upon. First, the disgust and unwillingness of these train-bands to be fellow soldiers with the aforesaid nation and to be on guard with them in the same guardhouse, and, on the other side, that the said nation was not admitted or counted among citizens, as regards trainbands or common citizens' guards, neither in the illustrious city of Amsterdam nor (to our knowledge) in any city in Netherland. But in order that the said nation may honestly be taxed for their freedom in that respect, it is directed by the director general and Council, to prevent further discontent, that the aforesaid nation shall, according to the usages of the renowned city of Amsterdam, remain exempt from the general training and guard duty, on condition that each male person over sixteen and under sixty years contribute for the aforesaid freedom toward the relief of the general municipal taxes sixty-five stivers (two cents equal one stiver) every month. And the military council of the citizens is hereby authorized and charged to carry this into effect until our further orders, and to collect, pursuant to the above, the aforesaid contribution once in every month, and, in case of refusal, to collect it by legal process. Thus done in Council at Fort Amsterdam.

"ON SUCH WHO PROFESS THE JEWISH RELIGION
SHALL BE NATURALIZED BY VIRTUE OF THIS ACT."
1740

This is the text of an Act (Anno 13 Geo. II, Cap. VII) allowing naturalization of Jews in the Colonies. The particular
references to the Jewish religion are interesting for the
contemporary reader.

An Act for naturalizing such foreign Protestants, and others therein
mentioned, as are settled or shall settle, in any of His Majesty's Colonies
in America.

Whereas the increase of People is a Means of advancing the Wealth and
Strength of any Nation or Country; And whereas many Foreigners and Strang-
ers from the Lenity of our Government, the Purity of our Religion, the
Benefit of our Laws, the Advantages of our Trade, and the Security of our
Property, might be induced to come and settle in some of His Majesty's
Colonies in America, if they were made Partakers of the Advantages and
Privileges which the natural born Subjects of this Realm do enjoy; Be it
therefore enacted by the King's Most Excellent Majesty, by and with the
Advice and Consent of the Lords Spiritual and Temporal, and Commons,
in this present Parliament assembled, and by the Authority of the same
That from and after the first Day of June in the Year of our Lord One thousand seven hundred and forty, all persons born out of the Legiance of His
Majesty, His Heirs or Successors, who have inhabited and resided, or shall
inhabit or reside for the Space of seven Years or more, in any of His Majesty's Colonies in America, and shall not have been absent out of some
of the said Colonies for a longer Space than two Months at any one time
during the said seven Years, and shall take and subscribe the Oaths, and
make, repeat and subscribe the Declaration appointed by an Act made in
the first Year of the Reign of His late Majesty King George the First, intituled, An Act for the further Security of His Majesty's Person and Government, and the Succession of the Crown in the Heirs of the late Princess
Sophia, being Protestants; and for extinguishing the Hopes of the pretended
Prince of Wales, his open and secret Abettors; or, being of the People called
Quakers, shall make and subscribe the Declaration of Fidelity, and take
and affirm the Effect of the Abjuration Oath, appointed and prescribed by
an Act made in the eighth Year of the Reign of His said late Majesty, intituled, An Act for granting the People called Quakers, such Forms of Af-
firmation or Declaration, as may remove the Difficulties which many of
them lie under; and also make and subscribe the Profession of his Christian
Belief, appointed and subscribed by an Act made in the first Year of the
Reign of their late Majesties King William and Queen Mary, intituled, An
Act for exempting Their Majesties Protestant Subjects from the Penalties

of certain Laws; before the Chief Judge, or other Judge of the Colony wherein such Persons respectively have so inhabited and ¯esided, or shall so inhabit and reside, shall be deemed, adjudged and taken to be His Majesty's
natural born Subjects of this Kingdom, to all Intents, Constructions and
Purposes, as if they and every of them had been or were born within this
Kingdom; which said Oath or Affirmation and Subscription of the said Declarations respectively, the Chief Judge or other Judge of every of the said
Colonies is hereby enabled and impowered to administer and take; and the
taking and subscribing of every such Oath or Affirmation, and the making,
repeating and subscribing of every such Declaration, shall be before such
Chief Judge or other Judge, in oper Court, between the Hours of nine and
twelve in the Forenoon; and shall be entered in the same Court, and also
in the Secretary's Office of the Colony wherein such Person shall so inhabit
and reside; and every Chief Judge or other Judges of every respective Colony, before whom such Oaths or Affirmation shall be taken and every such
Declaration shall be made, repeated and subscribed as aforesaid, is hereby required to make a due and proper entry thereof in a Book to be kept for
that Purpose in the said Court; for the doing whereof two Shillings and no
more shall be paid at each prepective place, under the Penalty and Forfeiture of ten Pounds of lawful Money of Great Britain for every Neglect or
Omission: And in like manner every Secretary of the Colony wherein any
Person shall so take the said Oaths or Affirmation, and make, repeat and
subscribe the said Declarations respectively, as aforesaid, is hereby required to make a due and proper Entry thereof in a Book to be kept for that
Purpose in his Office, upon Notification thereof to him by the Chief Judge
or other Judges of the same Colony, under the like Penalty and Forfeiture
for every such Neglect or Omission.

II. Provided always and be it enacted by the Authority aforesaid, That
no Person, of what Quality, Condition or Place soever, other than and except such of the People called Quakers as shall qualify themselves and be
naturalized by the ways and means hereinbefore mentioned, or such who
profess the Jewish Religion, shall be naturalized by virtue of this Act, unless such person shall have received the Sacrament of the Lord's Supper
in some Protestant and Reformed Congregation within this Kingdom of Great
Britain, or within some of the said Colonies in America, within three Months
next before his taking and subscribing the said Oaths, and making, repeating
and subscribing the said Declaration; and shall, at the time of his taking
and subscribing the said Declaration, produce a Certificate signed by the
Person administering the said Sacrament, and attested by two credible
Witnesses, whereof an Entry shall be made in the Secretary's Office of the
Colony, wherein such Person shall so inhabit and reside, as also in the
Court where said Oaths shall be so taken as aforesaid, without any Fee or
Reward.

III. And whereas the following Words are contained in the latter Part
of the Oath of Abjuration, videlicet, (upon the true Faith of a Christian):
And whereas the People professing the Jewish Religion may thereby be

prevented from receiving the Benefit of this Act; Be it further enacted by the Authority aforesaid, That whenever any Person professing the Jewish Religion shall present himself to take the said Oath of Abjuration in pursuance of this Act, the said Words (upon the true Faith of a Christian) shall be omitted out of the said Oath in administering the same to such Person, and the taking and subscribing the said Oath by such Person, professing the Jewish Religion, without the Words aforesaid, and the other Oaths appointed by the said Act in like manner as Jews were permitted to take the Oath of Abjuration, by an Act made in the tenth Year of the Reign of His late Majesty King George the First, intituled, An Act for explaining and amending an Act of the last Session of Parliament, intituled, An Act to oblige all Persons, being Papists, in that part of Great Britain called Scotland, and all persons in Great Britain, refusing or neglecting to take the Oaths appointed for the Security of His Majesty's Person and Government, by several Acts herein mentioned, to register their Names and real Estates; and for enlarging the time for taking the said Oaths, and making such Registers, and for allowing further time for the Inrolment of Deeds or Wills made by Papists, which have been omitted to be inrolled pursuant to an Act of the third Year of His Majesty's Reign; and also for giving Relief to Protestant Lesses, shall be deemed a sufficient taking of the said Oaths, in order to intitle such a person to the Benefit of being naturalized by virtue of this Act.

IV. And be it further enacted by the Authority aforesaid, That a Testimonial or Certificate under the Seal of any of the said Colonies, of any Persons having resided and inhabited for the Space of seven Years or more as aforesaid within the said Colonies or some of them, to be specified in such Certificate, together with the particular time of Residence in each of such respective Colonies (whereof the Colony under the Seal of which such Certificate shall be given to be one) and of his having taken and subscribed the said Declaration, and in case of a Quaker of his having made and subscribed the Declaration of Fidelity, and of his having taken and affirmed the Effect of the Abjuration Oath as aforesaid, and in the case of a Person professing the Jewish Religion, of his having taken the Oath of abjuration as aforesaid, within the same Colony, under the Seal whereof such Certificate shall be given as aforesaid, shall be deemed and taken to be a sufficient Testimony and Proof thereof, and of his being a natural born Subject of Great Britain, to all Intents and Purposes whatsoever, and as such shall be allowed in every Court within the Kingdoms of Great Britain and Ireland, and also in the said Colonies in America (Extended, 20 G. 2, c. 44, Sec. 1.)

V. And be it further enacted by the Authority aforesaid, That every Secretary of the said respective Colonies for the time being, shall and is hereby directed and required at the End of every Year, to be computed from the said first Day of June in the Year of Our Lord One thousand seven hundred and forty, to transmit and send over to the Office of the Commissioners for Trade and Plantations kept in the City of London or Westminster, a true and perfect List of the Names of all and every Person and Persons who have in that Year entitled themselves to the Benefit of this Act.

under the Penalty and Forfeiture of fifty Pounds of lawful Money of Great Britain for every Neglect or Omission: All which said lists so transmitted and sent over, shall, from Year to Year, be duly and regulary entered by the said Commissioners, in a Book or Books to be had and kept for that Purpose in the said Office, for publick View and inspection as Occasion shall require.

VI. Provided always, and it is hereby further enacted, That no Person who shall become a natural born Subject of this Kingdom by virtue of this Act, shall be of the Privy Council, or a Member of either House of Parliament, or capable of taking, having or enjoying any Office or Place of Trust within the Kingdoms of Great Britain or Ireland, either civil or military, or of having, accepting or taking any Grant from the Crown to himself, or to any other in trust for him, of any Lands, tenements or Heriditaments within the Kingdoms of Great Britain or Ireland; any Think hereinbefore contained to the contrary thereof in any wise notwithstanding. (Extended, 20 G. 2, c. 44. Persons naturalized by this Act capable of Offices, etc., civil and military, 13 G. 3, c. 25.)

"BEING A PERSON PROFESSING THE JEWISH RELIGION"
1741

This is probably the oldest naturalization certificate granted
to a Jew that is extant in North America.

George the Second, by the Grace of God of Great Britain, France, and
Ireland, King, Defender of the Faith, etc. To all whom these presents
shall come or may concern, greeting:

Know ye that it appears unto us by good testimony that Moses Lopez,
of the city of New York, merchant, being a person professing the Jewish
religion, hath resided and inhabited for the space of seven years and up-
wards within some of our colonies in America, and that the said Moses
Lopez, on the twenty-third day of October last, betwixt the hours of nine
and twelve in the forenoon of the same day, in our Supreme Court of Judi-
cature of our Province of New York, before our judges of our said court,
did take and subscribe the oaths of allegiance and supremacy and the abjuration oath, pursuant to the directions of an act of our Parliament of Great
Briatin, made and passed into the thirteenth year of our reign, entitled
"An Act for Naturalizing Such Foreign Protestants and Others therein Mentioned as Are Settled or Shall Settle in Any of His Majesty's Colonies in
America, " and that the said Moses Lopez's name is registered as a natural
born subject of Great Britain, both in our said Supreme Court and in our
Secretary's office of our said province, in books for that purpose severally
and particularly kept, pursuant to the directions of the aforesaid act.

In testimony whereof we have caused the great seal of our said Province
of New York to be hereunto affixed. Witness our trusty and well beloved
George Clarke, Esq., our Lieutenant Governor and Commander in Chief
of our Province of New York and the territories thereon depending in America, etc., the thirteenth day of April, Anno Domini 1741, and in the four-
teenth year of our reign.

George Joseph Moore, deputy secretary

"THE DISABILITY OF JEWS TO TAKE SEAT
AMONG THE REPRESENTATIVES"
1783

This petition was sent to the Council of Censors at Philadelphia in December, 1783, to protest a religious test oath
required for public office--a requirement maintained by a
number of states even after the Federal Constitution elim-
inated such a test for holding federal office.

To the honorable the Council of Censors, assembled agreeable to the
Constitution of the State of Pennsylvania.

The Memorial of Rabbi Gen. Sexias of the Synagogue of the Jews at
Philadelphia, Simon Nathan their Parnass or President, Asher Myers, Bernard Gratz, and Haym Solomon the Mahamad, or associates of their council,
in behalf of themselves and their brethren Jews, residing in Pennsylvania.

Most respectfully showeth.

That by the tenth section of the frame of government of this common-
wealth, it is ordered that each member of the general assembly of representatives of the freemen of Pennsylvania, before he takes his seat, shall
make and subscribe a declaration, which ends in these words, "I do acknowledge the Scriptures of the Old and New Testament to be given by divine in-
spiration," to which is added an assurance, that "no further or other religious test shall ever hereafter be required of any civil officer or magistrate in this state."

Your memorialists beg leave to observe, that this clause seems to limit
the civil rights of your citizens to one very special article of the creed;
whereas by the second paragraph of the declaration of the rights of the inhabitants, it is asserted without any other limitation than the professing the
existence of God, in plain words, "that no man who acknowledge the being
of a God can be justly deprived or abridged of any civil rights as a citizen,
on account of his religious sentiments." But certainly this religious test
deprives the Jews of the most eminent rights of freemen, solemnly ascer-
tained to all men who are not professed atheists.

Although the Jews in Pennsylvania are but a few in number, yet liberty
of the people in one country, and the declaration of the government thereof,
that these liberties are the rights of the people, may prove a powerful at-
tractive to men, who live under restraints in another country. Holland and
England have made valuable acquisitions of men who, for their religious
sentiments, were distressed in their own countries. And if Jews in Europe
or elsewhere, should incline to transport themselves to America, and would,
for reason of some certain advantage of the soil, climate, or the trade of
Pennsylvania, rather become inhabitants thereof, than of any other state;
yet the disability of Jews to take seat among the representatives of the people,

as worded by the said religious test, might determine their free choice to go to New York, or to any other of the United States of America, where there is no suchlike restraint laid upon the nation and religion of the Jews, as in Pennsylvania. Your memorialists cannot say that the Jews are particularly fond of being representatives of the people in assembly of civil officers and magistrates in the state but with great submission they apprehend that a clause in the constitution which disables them to be elected by their fellow citizens to represent them in assembly /is/ a stigma upon their nation and their religion, and it is inconsonant with the second paragraph of the said bill of rights; otherwise Jews are as fond of liberty as other religious societies can be, and it must create in them a displeasure, when they perceive that for their professed dissent to a doctrine, which is inconsistent with their religious sentiments, they should be excluded from the most important and honorable part of the rights of a free citizen.

Your memorialists beg further leave to represent, that in the religious books of the Jews, which are or may be in every man's hands, there are no such doctrines or principles established, as are inconsistent with the safety and happiness of the people of Pennsylvania, and that the conduct and behavior of the Jews in this and the neighboring states has always tallied with the great design of the Revolution; that the Jews of Charlestown, New York, Newport, and other posts occupied by the British troops, have distinguishedly suffered for their attachment to the Revolution principles; and their brethren at St. Eustatius, for the same cause, experienced the most severe resentments of the British commanders. The Jews of Pennsylvania in proportion to the number of their members, can count with any religious society whatsoever, the Whigs among either of them; they have served some of them in the Continental Army; some went out in the militia to fight the common enemy; all of them have cheerfully contributed to the support of the militia, and of the government of this state; they have no inconsiderable property in lands and tenements, but particularly in the way of trade, some more, some less, for which they pay taxes; they have, upon every plan formed for public utility, been forward to contribute as much as their circumstances would admit of; and as a nation or a religious society, they stand unimpeached of any matter whatsoever, against the safety and happiness of the people.

And your memorialists humbly pray, that if your Honors, from any other consideration than the subject of this address, should think proper to call a convention for revising the constitution, you would be pleased to recommend this to the notice of the convention.

The above was read and ordered on the table.

"THE CONFIDENCE THAT IS REPOSED IN ME
BY YOUR CONGREGATION"
1789

This letter from George Washington and addressed to the Hebrew Congregation of Savannah, Georgia, was in response to a letter of congratulation from the Congregation on his "appointment by unanimous approbation to the Presidential dignity of this country. "

I thank you with great sincerity for your congratulations on my appointment to the office, which I have the honor to hold by the unanimous choice of my fellow-citizens: and especially for the expressions which you are pleased to use in testifying the confidence that is reposed in me by your congregation.

As the delay which has naturally intervened between my election and your address has afforded an opportunity for appreciating the merits of the federal government, and for communicating your sentiments of its administration--I have rather to express my satisfaction than regret at a circumstance, which demonstrates (upon experiment) your attachment to the former as well as approbation of the latter.

I rejoice that a spirit of liberality and philanthropy is much more prevalent than it formerly was among the enlightened nations of the earth; and that your brethren will benefit thereby in proportion as it shall become still more extensive. Happily the people of the United States of America have, in many instances, exhibited examples worthy of imitation--the salutary influence of which will doubtless extend much farther, it gratefully enjoying those blessings of peace which (under favor of Heaven) have obtained by fortitude in war, they shall conduct themselves with reverence to the Deity, and charity towards their fellow-creatures.

May the same wonder-working Deity, who long since delivering the Hebrews from their Egyptian oppressors planted them in the promised land --whose providential agency has lately been conspicuous in establishing these United States as an independent nation--still continue to water them with the dews of Heaven and to make the inhabitants of every denomination participate in the temporal and spiritual blessings of that people whose God is Jehovah.

G. Washington

"PERMIT THE CHILDREN OF THE STOCK
OF ABRAHAM TO APPROACH YOU"
1790

The following is another letter to George Washington, this one addressed to him on the occasion of a visit to Newport, Rhode Island, from the Newport Congregation. Again, it reflects the concern of the Jews in America for perpetuating the freedom they have lacked abroad.

August 17

Sir:

Permit the Children of the Stock of Abraham to approach you with the most cordial affection and esteem for your person and merits--and to join with our fellow-citizens in welcoming you to New Port.

With pleasure we reflect on those days--those days of difficulty and danger, when the God of Israel, who delivered David from the Peril of the sword--shielded your head in the day of battle--and we rejoice to think that the same Spirit, who rested in the bosom of the greatly beloved Daniel, enabling him to preside over the Provinces of the Babylonish Empire, rests, and ever will rest upon you, enabling you to discharge the arduous duties of Chief Magistrate in these States.

Deprived as we have hitherto been of the invaluable rights of free citizens, we now, (with a deep sense of gratitude to the Almighty Disposer of all events) behold a Government erected by the Majesty of the People, which to bigotry gives no sanction, to persecution no assistance--but generously affording to all liberty of conscience, and immunities of citizenship--deeming every one, of whatever nation, tongue, or language equal parts of the great governmental machine. This so ample and extensive federal union whose basis is Philanthropy, mutual confidence, and great public virtue, we cannot but acknowledge to be the work of the Great God, who ruleth in the armies of Heaven, and among the inhabitants of the Earth, doing whatsoever seemeth him good.

For all the blessings of civil and religious liberty which we enjoy under an equal and benign administration we desire to send up our thanks to the Ancient of Days, the great Preserver of Men--beseeching him that the Angel who conducted our forefathers through the wilderness into the promised land, may graciously conduct you through all the dangers and difficulties of this mortal life--and when like Joshua full of days and full of honor, you are gathered to your Fathers, may you be admitted into the heavenly Paradise to partake of the water of life and the tree of immortality.

Done and signed by order of the Hebrew Congregation in New Port, Rhode Island, August 17, 1790.

Moses Sexias, Warden

"I GLORY IN BELONGING TO THAT PERSUASION"
1800

This is one of the few political documents of early American Jewry. It is a letter written by Benjamin Nones in response to a slandering piece about his religion and economic status which appeared in the Federalist newspaper, Gazette of the United States. A copy of the response was also sent to the Republican newspaper, The Philadelphia Aurora, since Nones correctly anticipated that the former would not publish his letter.

TO THE PRINTER OF THE GAZETTE
OF THE UNITED STATES

Sir,

I hope, if you take the liberty of inserting calumnies against individuals, for the amusement of your readers, you will at least have so much regard to justice, as to permit the injured through the same channel that conveyed the slander, to appeal to the public in self defence.--I expect of you therefore, to insert this reply to your ironical reporter of the proceedings at the meeting of the republican citizens of Philadelphia, contained in your gazette of the fifth instant; so far as I am concerned in that statement. --I am no enemy Mr. Wayne to wit; nor do I think the political parties have much right to complain, if they enable the public to laugh at each others expence, provided it be managed with the same degree of ngenuity, and some attention to truth and candour. But your reporter of the proceedings at that meeting is as destitute of truth and candour, as he is of ingenuity, and I think, I can shew, that the want of prudence of this Mr. Marplot, in his slander upon me, is equally glaring with his want of wit, his want of veracity, his want of decency, and his want of humanity.

I am accused of being a Jew; of being a Republican; and of being Poor.

I am a Jew. I glory in belonging to that persuasion, which even its opponents, whether Christian, or Mahomedan, allow to be of divine origin --of that persuasion on which christianity itself was originally founded, and must ultimately rest--which has preserved its faith secure and undefiled, for near three thousand years--whose votaries have never murdered each other in religious wars, or cherished the theological hatred so general, so inextinguishable among those who revile them. A persuasion, whose, patient followers, have endured for ages the pious cruelties of Pagans, and of christians, and persevered in the unoffending practice of their rites and ceremonies, amidst poverties and privations--amidst pains, penalties, confiscations, banishments, tortures, and deaths, beyond the example of any other sect, which the page of history has hitherto recorded.

To be of such a persuasion, is to me no disgrace; though I well understand the inhuman language of bigotted contempt, in which your reporter
by attempting to make me ridiculous, as a Jew, has made himself detest-
able, whatever religious persuasion may be dishonored by his adherence.

But I am a Jew. I am so--and so were Abraham, and Isaac, and Moses
and the prophets, and so too were Christ and his apostles, I feel no disgrace in ranking with such society, however, it may be subject to the illiberal buffoonery of such men as your correspondents.

I am a Republican! Thank God, I have not been so heedless, and so
ignorant of what has passed, and is now passing in the political world. I
have not been so proud or so prejudiced as to renounce the cause for which
I have fought, as an American throughout the whole of the revolutionary
war, in the militia of Charleston, and in Polafkey's legion, I fought in almost every action which took place in Carolina, and in the disastrous af-
fair of Savannah, shared the hardships of that sanguinary day, and for three
and twenty years I felt no disposition to change my political, any more than
my religious principles.--And which in spite of the witling scribblers of
aristocracy, I shall hold sacred until death as not to feel the ardour of
republicanism.--Your correspondent, Mr. Wayne cannot have known what
it is to serve his country from principle in time of danger and difficulties
at the expence of his health and his peace, of his pocket and his person,
as I have done; or he would not be as he is, a pert reviler of those who
have so done--as I do not suspect you Mr. Wayne, of being the author of
the attack on me. I shall not enquire what share you or your relations had
in establishing the liberties of your country. On religious grounds I am a
republican. Kingly government was first conceded to the foolish complaints
of the Jewish people, as a punishment and a curse; and so it was to them
until their dispersion, and so it has been to every nation, who have been
as foolishly tempted to submit to it. Great Britain has a king, and her
enemies need not wish her the sword, the pestilence, and the famine.

In the history of the Jews, are contained the earliest warnings against
kingly government, as any one may know who has read the fable of Abi-
melick, or the exhortations of Samuel. But I do not recommend them to
your reporter, Mr. Wayne. To him the language of truth and soberness
would be unintelligible.

I am a Jew, and if for no other reason, for that reason am I a republican. Among the pious priesthood of church establishments, we are com-
passionately ranked with Turks, Infidels and Heretics. In the monarchies
of Europe, we are hunted from society--stigmatized as unworthy of common civility, thrust out as it were from the converse of men; objects of
mockery and insult to froward children, the butts of vulgar wit, and low
buffoonery, such as your correspondent Mr. Wayne is not ashamed to set
us an example of. Among the nations of Europe we are inhabitants every
where--but Citizens no where unless in Republics. Here, in France, and
in the Batavian Republic alone, we are treated as men and brethren. In
republics we have rights, in monarchies we live but to experience wrongs.

And why? because we and our forefathers have <u>not</u> sacrificed our principles to our interest, or earned an exemption from pain and poverty, by the dir-eliction of our religious duties, no wonder we are objects of derision to those, who have no principles, moral or religious, to guide their conduct.

How then can a Jew but be a Republican? in America particularly. Unfeeling & ungrateful would he be, if he were callous to the glorious and benevolent cause of the difference between his situation in this land of free-dom, and among the proud and privileged law givers of Europe.

But I am <u>poor</u>, I am so, my family also is large, but soberly and de-cently brought up. They have not been taught to revile a christian, because his religion is not <u>so old</u> as theirs. They have not been taught to mock even at the errors of good intention, and conscientious belief. I hope they will always leave this to men as unlike themselves, as I hope I am to your scurrilous correspondent.

I know that to purse proud aristocracy poverty is a crime, but it may sometimes be accompanied with honesty even in a Jew. I was a bankrupt some years ago. I obtained my certificate and I was discharged from my debt. Having been more successful afterwards, I called my creditors together, and eight years afterwards unsolicited I discharged all my old debts, I offered interest which was refused by my creditors, and they gave me under their hands without any solicitations of mine, as a testimonial of the fact (to use their own language) as a tribute due to my honor and honesty. This testimonial was signed by Messrs. J. Ball, W. Wister, George Meade, J. Philips, C. G. Paleske, J. Bispham, J. Cohen, Robert Smith, J. H. Leuffer, A. Kuhn, John Stille, S. Pleasants, M. Woodhouse, Thomas Harrison, M. Boraef, E. Laskey, and Thomas Allibone, &c.

I was discharged by the insolvent act, true, because having the amount of my debts owing to me from the French Republic, the differences between France and America have prevented the recovery of what was due to me, in time to discharge what was due to my creditors. Hitherto it has been the fault of the political situation of the two countries, that my creditors are not paid; when peace shall enable me to receive what I am entitled to it will be my fault if they are not fully paid.

This is a long defence Mr. Wayne, but you have called it forth, and therefore, I hope you at least will not object to it. The Public will not judge who is the proper object of ridicule and contempt, your facetious reporter, or

Your Humble Servant,

BENJAMIN NONES.

"THAT THE LEGISLATURE WILL LOOK WITH AN EQUAL EYE"
1806

> In spite of the doctrine of separation of church and state as
> written in the Constitution, the practice of state aid to pa-
> rochial schools continued from the colonial period into the
> first years of the new Republic. This petition was prepared
> by DeWitt Clinton for Congregation Shearith Israel of New
> York City. Clinton's great influence assured approval.

The petition of the trustees of the Congregation of Shearith Israel in
the city of New York most respectfully represent:

That from the year 1793 a school has been supported from the funds
of the said congregation for the education of their indigent children. That
on the 8th of April, 1801, certain school monies were distributed among
seven charity schools of the said citys upported by religious societies. That
the free school of the Roman Catholic Church and that of your memorialists
were overlooked in this benevolent distribution.

That on the 21st of March, 1806, a law was passed placing the school
of the former on the same footing as the others. That your memorialists
also made application to the legislature, but did not succeed, owing, as they
presume, to the pressure of business.

Your memorialists, fully persuaded that the legislature will look with
an equal eye upon all occupations of people who conduct themselves as good
and faithful citizens, and conscious that nothing has been omitted on their
part to deserve the same countenance and encouragement which has been
exhibited to others, do most respectfully pray your honorable body to extend
the same relief to their charity school which has been granted to all others
in this city.

"WE WISH NOT TO ABANDON THE INSTITUTIONS OF MOSES, BUT TO UNDERSTAND AND OBSERVE THEM"
1824

This memorial is the first document dealing with the movement to Reform Judaism in the United States. It was rejected by the Congregation Beth Elohim in Charleston, S. C., to which it was submitted by a small group of 47 congregants. The Reformed Society of Israelites was founded in the following year.

Gentlemen,

The memorial of the undersigned, showeth unto your honourable body, that they have witnessed with deep regret, the apathy and neglect which have been manifested towards our holy religion. As inheritors of the true faith, and always proud to be considered by the world as a portion of "God's chosen people," they have been pained to perceive the gradual decay of that system of worship, which, for ages past, peculiarly distinguished us from among the nations of the earth. Not unmindful, however, of the various causes which regulate human conduct; and at the same time, unwilling to shield themselves from any censure to which their actions may justly entitle them, they have ingenuously investigated the reasons which may have led them from the Synagogue, and are now seriously impressed with the belief, that certain defects which are apparent in the present system of worship, are the sole causes of the evils complained of.

In pointing out these defects, however, your memorialists seek no other end, than the future welfare and respectability of the nation. As members of the great family of Israel, they cannot consent to place before their children examples which are only calculated to darken the mind, and withhold from the rising generation the more rational means of worshipping the true God.

It is to this, therefore, your memorialists would, in the first place, invite the serious attention of your honourable body. By causing the Hasan, or reader, to repeat in English such part of the Hebrew prayers as may be deemed necessary, it is confidently believed that the congregation generally would be more forcibly impressed with the necessity of Divine Worship, and the moral obligations which they owe to themselves and their Creator; While such a course, would lead to more decency and decorum during the time they are engaged in the performance of religious duties. It is not every one who has the means, and many have not the time, to acquire a knowledge of the Hebrew language, and consequently to become enlightened in the principles of Judaism; What then is the course pursued in all religious societies for the purpose of disseminating the peculiar tenets of their faith

among the poor and uninformed? The principles of their religion are ex-
pounded to them from the pulpit in language that they understand; for instance, in the Catholic, the German and the French Protestant Churches:
by this means the ignorant part of mankind attend their places of worship
with some profit to their morals, and even improvement to their minds;
they return from them with hearts turned to piety, and with feelings elevated by their sacred character. In this consists the beauty of religion,--
when men are invoked by its divine spirit, to the practice of virtue and
morality.

These results, it is respectfully submitted, would be sufficient of themselves to induce the alterations requested. But your memorialists cannot
fail to impress upon the minds of your honourable body, the singular advantages this practice would produce upon the habits and attention of the
younger branches of the congregation; besides the necessity of good be-
haviour, which the solemnity of the service should impose, they would become gradually better acquainted with the nature of our creed, the principal features which distinguish the Jew from every other religious denomination, and the meaning, and the reason, of our various forms and ceremonies. Believing, at the same time, that the above views of what is in-
dispensable to the preservation of our faith, will meet with the approbation of every reflecting and liberal mind--they repeat, that they are actuated
by no other motive, than to see our Synagogue in a better, a more whole-
some, and a more respectable state of discipline; to see it elicit that regard from Jew and Gentile, which its great character deserves, and should
always command; and finally, not to destroy long standing institutions, but
to accommodate them to the progress of time, and change of situation and
circumstances.

With regard to such parts of the service as it is desired should under-
go this change, your memorialists would strenuously recommend that the
most solemn portions be retained, and everything superfluous excluded;
and that the principal parts, and if possible all that is read in <u>Hebrew,</u>
should also be read in <u>English,</u> (that being the language of the country,)
so as to enable every member of the congregation fully to understand each
part of the service. In submitting this article of our memorial to the consideration of your honourable body, your memorialists are well aware of
the difficulties with which they must contend, before they will be enabled
to accomplish this desirable end; but while they would respectfully invite
the attention of your honourable body to this part of their memorial, they
desire to rest the propriety and expediency of such a measure, solely upon
the <u>reason</u> by which it may be maintained. Your memorialists would further
submit to your honourable body whether, in the history of the civilized
world, there can be found a single parallel of a people, addressing the <u>Cre-
ator</u> in a language not understood <u>by that people</u>? It is indeed surprising,
that heretofore no innovation has even been <u>attempted,</u> although it is readily
admitted your honourable body may boast of many very enlightened, liberal
and intelligent members.

Your memorialists would next call the particular attention of your honourable body to the absolute necessity of abridging the service generally. They have reflected seriously upon its present length, and are confident that this is one of the principal causes why so much of it is hastily and improperly hurried over. This must be evident to every reflecting mind, when it is seen, that notwithstanding the evil complained of, the service of the Sabbath, for instance, continues until <u>twelve</u> o'clock, although usually commencing at <u>nine</u>. It is therefore manifest, that, according to the prayer of your memorialists, should the service be in future conducted with due solemnity, and in a slow, distinct, and impressive tone, its length would certainly occupy the attention of the congregation, until two o'clock if not later.

The <u>Offerings</u> will next command the attention of your honourable body; and upon this part of our memorial, we would respectfully crave the favour of a patient hearing, while we clearly set forth the entire uselessness and impropriety of this custom. In the first place, your memorialists earnestly protest against the unwise and absurd practice of rendering in the Spanish language, any offerings which may be intended to benefit the Synagogue, or which may be otherwise identified with our holy religion. Besides the free scope which the practice of offering in a language understood by few, affords to mischievous and designing men to pollute the holy altars by gratifying their evil intentions--we certainly think it highly inconsistent to select for this very purpose, the language of a people from whom we have suffered, and continue to suffer, so much persecution. But forgetting for a moment this consideration, your memorialists would further suggest to your honourable body, whether the arrangement recently made in the financial transactions of the congregation, would not altogether supercede the necessity of any offerings whatever? This is most seriously and strenuously desired by your memorialists, because they are prepared to show, by an act of your own body, that the practice of offering is not the result of any imperious necessity, but merely intended as an idle and absurd indulgence. By the 11th Article of the Constitution of your honourable body, it is provided, that such offerings as are made by any member of the congregation, shall, at the end of the year, be <u>deducted out of the amount of his annual subscription, as well as that of his wife, if he be a married man</u>. According to this part of the Constitution, a revenue is <u>created independent of the offerings which are subsequently made and deducted out of the amount of subscription at the end of the year</u>. Your memorialists would, therefore, inquire, wherein exists the necessity, under this arrangement, of any offerings whatever? How, and in what manner, the support of the congregation <u>depends</u> upon them? and, in a word, whether the above article is not a tacit admission by your Constitution, that so much of the offerings as may amount to the annual subscription of a member, was never intended as a means of supporting the congregation, inasmuch, as the whole amount is <u>already</u> anticipated long before a single offering is made! In fact, many persons, when their amount of assessment is exhausted in offerings, are induced to go out and remain in the Synagogue yard, to prevent being compelled to offer against their will,--a practice irregular, indecorous, and highly to be censured, --because it sets an ill example to our children, and draws upon us in the eyes of strangers.

Your memorialists are aware, it may be said, that some few subscribers offer _more_ than the amount of their annual subscription. But to this it may be answered, that it is certainly not difficult for the general body, in their wisdom and discretion, to devise some means equally profitable to the congregation, and at the same time, as well calculated to meet the views of the _liberal_, without resorting to a practice, which only interrupts the worship of God, and s productive of so little good. Your memorialists therefore respectfully suggest, that the addition in numbers to your body, which it is expected will shortly take place, will greatly aid in the funds, and serve as an additional reason why the offerings should be abolished; but as a further inducement for their entire abolishment, your memorialists would respectfully recommend, the propriety and expediency of addressing to the understanding of the people, and more particularly the younger branches of the congregation, appropriate discourses, in the place and at the very time the offerings are usually made.

According to the present mode of reading the Parasa, it affords to the hearer neither instruction nor entertainment, unless he be competent to read as well as comprehend the Hebrew language. But if, like all other ministers, our reader would make a chapter or verse the subject of an English discourse once a week, at the expiration of the year the people would, at all events, know something of that religion which at present they so little regard.

It is also worthy of observation, that a number of Israelites, whom it should be the special care of your honourable body to bring back under your immediate protection and influence, are now wandering gradually from the true God, and daily losing those strong ties which bind every pious man to the faith of his fathers! In these individuals, your honourable body have fair subjects for the holy work of reformation; by moulding your present form of worship to suit their comprehensions, you will instantly receive them among you; they will collect under your especial care and guardianship; they will aid in the pecuniary resources of your holy institutions; and if, from among the whole number now scattered about our city and state, either through irreligion, through disabilities imposed, or any other cause, you are enabled to make but one convert, it will add much to those laudable ends which it should be the principal desire of your honourable body to accomplish. It should also be remembered that while other sects are extending the means of Divine Worship to the remotest quarters of the habitable globe--while they are making the most zealous efforts to bring together the scattered of their flock, offering the most flattering inducements to all denominations--we, who may be termed the mere remnant of a great nation, are totally disregarding the fairest opportunities of increasing our own numbers, and at the same time neglecting the brightest prospects of enlarging our resources, and effectually perpetuating our national character.

Your memorialists trust, that they have been perfectly understood by the foregoing observations, that they entirely disclaim any idea of wishing to abolish such ceremonies as are considered land-marks to distinguish the Jew from the Gentile; they are wholly influenced by a warm zeal to preserve the principles of Judaism n their utmost purity and vigour, and to see the present and the future generations of Israelites enlightened on the subject of their holy religion, so as by understanding, they may learn the nature of its Divine source, and appreciate its holy precepts; that they would not wish to shake the firmness of any man's faith, or take from his devotion towards it; that they will always fervently and zealously support it as the first and most ancient of religions.

The alterations above submitted, being all your memorialists can in reason and moderation require, they would beg leave, in concluding, to bring to the notice of your honourable body, the reformation which has been recently adopted by our brethren in Holland, Germany and Prussia. The following is an extract from a German paper entitled the "Frankfort Journal."

"The functions relative to Divine Service, such as the rite of taking the Law out of the Ark, the promulgation of the Law, etc., shall no longer be sold by auction in the Synagogue. The Rabbis, and the Elders of the Synagogue, (the first in their discourses) must endeavor to put an end to the custom of see-sawing during the prayers, and to that of repeating the prayers in too loud a voice; all profane tunes during the Divine Service are prohibited. The ceremony of striking the impious Haman at the festival of Purim, is most strictly prohibited. Children below the age of five years are not to be taken to the Synagogue. All unsuitable pleasantries, in which the young people sometimes indulge in the Synagogues on the eve of some festivals, or on the festivals themselves, as well as the distribution of sweetmeats by the women to each in the Synagogues, are strictly forbidden. Some of the religious ceremonies must be accompanied by a German discourse (that being the vernacular) on a Hebrew text, in which the meaning of these solemnities shall be explained, and on the Sabbath a discourse shall be held in German in every Synagogue after the reading of the prescribed passage of the Law, and a chapter of the Prophets."

Thus, from the above extract, it appears, that no climes, nor even tyranny itself, can forever fetter or control the human mind; and that even amidst the intolerance of Europe, our brethren have anticipated the free citizens of America in the glorious work of reformation; Let us then hasten to the task with harmony and good fellowship. We wish not to overthrow, but to rebuild; we wish not to destroy, but to reform and revise the evils complained of; we wish not to abandon the institutions of Moses, but to understand and observe them; in fine, we wish to worship God, not as slaves

of bigotry and priestcraft, but as the enlightened descendants of that chosen
race, whose blessings have been scattered throughout the land of Abraham,
Isaac and Jacob.

And your memorialists will ever pray.

(Signed by forty-seven Israelites of the City of Charleston.)

"NO JEWS WANTED HERE"
1849

Jews faced unequal opportunity in employment. This editorial makes an early distinction between public and private discrimination. It appeared in the N.Y. Sun.

A Bohemian writes to ask us what we meant by saying in our article yesterday on the secret of success, that in this country all are equally encouraged and protected; for he says he is a Hebrew by race, though a naturalized citizen, and that certain persons, tradesmen, in advertising in a journal of this city for a number of shade painters, put in as an exception, 'No Jews wanted here.' Bohemian, being a Jew, and a shade painter, thinks the doctrine of equal encouragement and protection don't work here. We did not expect any such interpretation. We meant simply that the government and institutions of this country hold out the same inducements and chances to every citizen--in thus much and thus far they are equally protected and encouraged. If individuals, or members of different races and clans will disagree and battle with each other, the quarrel is theirs, and the more pitiable and shameful it is, to him who draws the weapon first and uses it furthest. We apprehend the spirit of our institutions and government is often more liberal and generous than that of many individuals who enjoy its blessings and who ought to imitate its example.

"IT CANNOT BE SAID THAT THE JEWS HAVE FORMED
ANY DENOMINATIONAL OPINION ON THE SUBJECT
OF AMERICAN SLAVERY."
1853

This excerpt from a report made by an abolitionist group
indicates the opinion of that group (The American & Foreign
Anti-Slavery Society) regarding the position of American
Jewry in the anti-slavery movement up to this point in the
history of that issue.

The Jews

The Jews of the United States have never taken any steps whatever with
regard to the Slavery question. As citizens, they deem it their policy "to
have every one choose which ever side he may deem best to promote his
own interests and the welfare of his country." They have no organization
of an ecclesiastical body to represent their general views; no General Assembly, or its equivalent. The American Jews have two newspapers, but
they do not interfere in any discussion which is not material to their religion. It cannot be said that the Jews have formed any denominational opinion
on the subject of American slavery. Some of the Jews, who reside in slave
States, have refused to have any property in man, or even to have any slaves
about them. They do not believe that any thing analogous to slavery, as it
exists in this country, ever prevailed among the ancient Israelites. But
they profess to believe that "the belief of Abraham, enlarged by Moses, and
now acknowledged by the Jews, is one of purity and morality, and one which
presentst he strongest possible supports for civil society, <u>especially a government based upon principles of equality and liberty of the person!</u> They
believe that the coming of the King Messiah will be the signal for universal
peace, universal freedom, universal knowledge, and universal worship of
the One Eternal."
    The objects of so much mean prejudice and unrighteous oppression as
the Jews have been for ages, surely they, it would seem, more than any
other denomination, ought to be the enemies of CASTE, and the friends of
UNIVERSAL FREEDOM.

"NOT A SINGLE JEW REQUIRING TEMPORARY RELIEF"
1854

The following newspaper editorial from the Washington
Sentinel of May 21, 1854, represents a prevailing view of
the Jews in the United States in the mid-19th century.

"Not a single Jew requiring temporary relief." Such is the report of
missionaries and colporteurs appointed by the New York Society for the
Amelioration of the Condition of the Jews in that city--Exchange paper.

Such would be the report in almost every city in the United States--we
might say in the world. This ancient race can boast that there are among
them fewer paupers and fewer criminals than any other race can exhibit.
When the history of the Jews is considered; when the hardships, trials, and
persecutions to which they have been subjected are borne in mind; it is indeed wonderful that they should have retained most of those better traits
that dignify and adorn civilized man. Oppressed by rigorous laws in every
country, defrauded, insulted, beaten, and spit upon by every people, it is
surprising that they have not been rendered fierce, resentful, and malignant.
It is surprising, too, that they should have retained their elasticity and
their business capacity.

Denied citizenship in most of the countries of Christendom, debarred
from the pursuits of ambition, incapable of holding offices of honor and
profit, kicked and cuffed by all mankind, they have bent all their energies
to one object, and that the accumulation of money. But even money, when
obtained, attracted to them a more rigorous persecution. That persecution, which broke their spirit and destroyed their manliness, served at the
same time to quicken their wits, sharpen their sagacity, and drive them
into a closer and firmer brotherhood. With no friends in the wide world,
they learned to cling with affectionate tenacity to one another. The wit that
under their persecutions enabled them to accumulate money, also enabled
them to conceal their treasures from the vigilant eyes of their enemies.
Many of them, even in the Dark Ages, were princes in wealth, but very
babies in spirit and helplessness.

But, happily for this ancient race--this, the oldest and the purest of
earth's aristocracy, for they are descended from the kings, prophets, and
nobles of Israel--happily for them, as the world became enlightened and
Christianized, persecution relaxed its iron hand, and privileges were ac-
corded to them.

Now, in this golden age, they are allowed to come and go as they will.
They can choose their abiding places as inclination may dictate. But the
liberal institutions of this favored land induce many to live amongst us.
The Jew here has the same privileges--social, religious, and political--

that any other class enjoys. He exercises the right of suffrage. He is eligible to office. All the professions that ambition delights in, all the pursuits that the love of gain inclines to, are open to the Jew as to any other man.

The habit of acquisitiveness which seems to be natural, but which may be the result of oppression, still clings to them. They seldom enter the professions. They seldom turn their attention to politics. They seldom till the soil. They seem to prefer trade and commerce.

Yet some of the finest lawyers and orators that this country can boast of belong to the ancient Jewish race. We did not, however, design writing an essay on this subject. That would be better adapted to a review than a journal like ours. We only intended to call attention to the fact developed in the statistics of the country, that the Jews are among our best citizens. If we enter a penitentiary or prison of any description, the marked face of the Israelite is rarely to be seen within its walls. Such a thing as a Jew in a poorhouse was hardly ever known. Jews seldom commit murder or any of those crimes and offenses that are marked by violence and passion. The offenses committed by them, and they are of rare occurrence, are frauds, and small larcenies. A Jewish beggar is a thing almost unknown.

But they are generally regarded as a close and coldhearted race. That they are so towards the outside world, is perhaps true; for their bounties, their charities, and benevolence are rarely extended beyond their race and brotherhood. But none can deny that they take care of their poor, comfort their afflicted, and relieve their distressed. In this they set an example worthy of all imitation. They are among the best, most orderly, well disposed of our citizens.

"I DESIRE THAT MY MORTAL REMAINS BE BURIED IN THE JEWISH CEMETERY IN NEW PORT RHODE ISLAND."
1854

Judah Touro was one of the earliest of well-known American philanthropists. His beneficiaries, as described in his will, included all religions, creeds, and races, thereby setting a tradition which has remained with Jewish philanthropists to the present day.

JUDAH TOURO
UNITED STATES OF AMERICA
State of Louisiana, City of New Orleans

Be it Known that on this Sixth day of January, in the year of our Lord One Thousand, Eight Hundred and Fifty Four, and of the Independence of the United States of America the Seventy Eighth and a quarter before Ten O' Clock A.M.

Before me, Thomas Layton, a notary Public, in and for the city of New Orleans, aforesaid duly commissioned and sworn, and in Presence of Messieurs, Jonathan Montgomery, Henry Shepherd Jr. and George Washington Lee competent witnesses residing in said city and hereto expressly required

Personally appeared Mr. Judah Touro of this City, Merchant, whom I the said Notary and said witnesses found setting in a room at his residence No. 128, Canal Street, Sick of body, but sound in mind, memory and Judgment as did appear to me, the said Notary and to said witnesses. And the said Judah Touro requested me, the notary, to receive his last will or Testament, which he dictated to me, Notary, as follows, to wit & in presence of said witnesses.

1st. I declare that I have no forced heirs.

2nd. I desire that my mortal remains be buried in the Jewish Cemetery in New Port Rhode Island, as soon as practicable after my decease.

3d. I nominate and appoint my trusty and Esteemed friends Rezin Davis Shepherd of Virginia, Aaron Keppel Josephs of New Orleans, Gershom Kursheedt of New Orleans, and Pierre Andre Destrac Cazenave of New Orleans, my Testamentary Executors and the detainers of my Estate, making, however, the following distinction between my said Executors, to wit: to the said Aaron Keppel Josephs, Gershom Kursheedt and Pierre Andre Destrac Cazenave, I give and bequeath to each one separately the sum of Ten Thousand dollars, which legacies, I intend respectively not only as tokens of remembrance of those esteemed friends, but also in consideration of all Services they may have hitherto rendered me, and in lieu of the commissions to which they would be entitled hereafter in the capacity of Testamentary Executors as aforesaid. And as regards any other designated Executors, say my dear old and devoted friend the said Rezin Davis Shepherd to whom, under Divine Providence, I was greatly indebted for the preservation of my life, when I was wounded on the 1st of January 1815, I hereby appoint and institute him, the said Rezin Davis Shepherd, after the payment of my particular legacies and the debts of my succession, the Universal Legatee of the rest and residue of my estate, moveable and immoveable.

In case of the death, absence, or inhability (sic) to act of one or more of my said Executors, I hereby empower the remaining Executor or Executors to act in carrying out the provisions of this my last Will, and in the event or default of any one or more of my said Executors before my own demise, then and in that case, it is my intention that the heirs or legal representatives of those who may depart this life before my own death, Shall inherit in their Stead the legacies hereinabove respectively made to them.

4th. I desire that all leases on my property and which may be in force at the time of my demise, Shall be faithfully executed until the Same Shall have expired.

5th. I desire that all the Estate Real, Personal and mixed, of which I may die possessed, Shall be disposed of in the manner directed by this my last will or Testament.

6th. I give and bequeath to the Hebrew Congregation of the (")Dispersed of Judah" of the City of New Orleans, all that certain property situated in Bourbon Street immediately adjoining their Synagogue, being the present School house and the residence of the Said Mr. Gershom Kursheedt, the same purchased by me from the Bank of Louisiana; and also to the said Hebrew Congregation, the Two adjoining brick Houses purchased from the heirs of David Urquhart, the revenue of said property to be applied to the founding and support of the Hebrew School connected, with Said congregation, as well to the defraying of the Salary of their Reader or Minister, Said Property to be conveyed accordingly by my said Executors to said congregation, with all necessary restrictions.

7th. I give and bequeath to found the (")Hebrew Hospital of New Orleans" The entire property purchased for me, at the succession sale of the late C. Paulding upon which property the Building now Known as the "Touro Infirmary" is situated: The said contemplated Hospital to be organized according to law, as a charitable institution for the relief of the Indigent Sick, by my Executors and such other persons as they may associate with them conformably with the laws of Louisiana.

8th. I give and bequeath to the Hebrew Benevolent Association of New Orleans Five Thousand Dollars.

9th. I give and bequeath to the Hebrew Congregation "Shangarar Chased" of New Orleans Five Thousand Dollars.

10th. I give and bequeath to the Ladies Benevolent Society of New Orleans, the Sum of Five Thousand dollars.

11th. I give and bequeath to the Hebrew Foreign Mission Society of New Orleans, Five Thousand Dollars.

12th. I give and bequeath to the Orphans Home Asylum of New Orleans, the sum of Five Thousand Dollars.

13th. I give and bequeath to the Society for the relief of Destitute Orphan Boys in the Fourth District, Five Thousand Dollars.

14th. I give and bequeath to the St. Anna's Asylum for the relief of destitute females and children, the sum of Five Thousand Dollars.

15th. I give and bequeath to the New Orleans Female Orphan Asylum at the corner of Camp and Prytania Streets, Five Thousand Dollars.

16th. I give and bequeath to the St. Mary's Catholic Boys Asylum of which my old & esteemed friend Mr. Anthony Rasch is chairman of its Executive Committee, the sum of Five Thousand Dollars.

17th. I give and bequeath to the Milne Asylum of New Orleans, Five Thousand Dollars.

18th. I give and bequeath to the Fireman's charitable Association of New Orleans, Four Thousand Dollars.

19th. I give and bequeath to the Seamen's Home in the First District of New Orleans Five Thousand Dollars.

20th. I give and bequeath for the purpose of establishing an Alms House, in the City of New Orleans, and with the view of contributing as far as possible to the prevention of mendicity in said city, the sum of Eighty Thousand Dollars (say $80,000); and I desire that the Alms House, thus contemplated, shall be organized according to law; and further it is my desire that after my Executors Shall have legally organized & established said contemplated Alms House and appointed proper persons to administer and controll the direction of its affairs, then such persons legally so appointed and their successors in office, conjointly with the Mayor of the City of New Orleans and his successors in office shall have the perpetual direction and controll thereof.

21st. I give and bequeath to the City of New Port in the State of Rhode Island, the Sum of Ten Thousand Dollars, on condition that the said sum be expended in the purchase and improvement of the property in Said City, Known as the "Old Stone Mill(")" to be Kept as a public Park or Promenade ground.

22d. I give and bequeath to the Red Wood library of New Port aforesaid, for Books & Repairs Three Thousand Dollars.

23. I give and bequeath to the Hebrew Congregation Oharbay Shalome of Boston Massachusetts Five Thousand dollars.

24. I give and bequeath to the Hebrew Congregation of Hartford Connecticut Five Thousand dollars.

25. I give and bequeath to the Hebrew Congregation of New Haven Connecticut Five Thousand dollars.

26. I give and bequeath to the North American Relief Society for the Indigent Jews. of Jerusalem Palestine of the City and State of New York (Sir Moses Montefiore of London, their agent) Ten Thousand Dollars. Say ($10,000.)

27. It being my earnest wish to co-operate with the said Sir Moses Montefiore of London, Great Britain, in endeavouring (sic) to ameliorate the condition of our unfortunate Jewish brethern (sic) in the Holy Land, and to secure to them the inestimable privilege of worshipping the Almighty according to our Religion, without molestation, I therefore give and bequeath the sum of Fifty Thousand Dollars to be paid by my Executors for said object through the said Sir Moses Montefiore, in such manner as he may advise as best calculated to promote the aforesaid objects, and in case of any legal or other difficulty or impediment in the way of carrying said bequest into effect, according to my intentions, then and in that case, I desire that the said sum of Fifty Thousand dollars be invested by my Executors in the foundation of a Society in the City of New Orleans Similar in its objects to the North American Relief Society for the Indigent Jews of Jerusalem, Palestine, of the City of New York, to which I have before referred in this my last Will.

28. It is my wish and desire that the Institutions to which I have already alluded in making this Will, as well as those to which in the further course of making this Will, I shall refer, Shall not be disqualified from inheriting my legacies to them respectively made for reason of not being Incorporated & thereby qualified to inherit by law, but on the contrary, I desire that the parties interested in such Institutions and my Executors Shall facilitate their Organization as soon after my decease as possible, & thus render them duly qualified by law to inherit in the premises according to my wishes.

29. I give and bequeath to the Jews Hospital Society of the City and State of New York Twenty Thousand Dollars.

30. I give and bequeath to the Hebrew Benevolent Society Mashebat Nafesh of New York, Five Thousand dollars.

31. I give and bequeath to the Hebrew Benevolent Society Gimelet Chased of New York Five Thousand Dollars.

32. I give and bequeath to the Talmueh (sic) Torah School fund attached to the Hebrew Congregation Sheareth Israel of the City of New York and to said Congregation Thirteen Thousand Dollars.

33. I give and bequeath to the Educational Institute of the Hebrew Congregation Briai Jeshurum (sic) of the City of New York the sum of Three Thousand Dollars.

34. I give and bequeath to the Hebrew Congregation Shangarai Tefila of New York Three Thousand Dollars.

35. I give and bequeath to the Ladies Benevolent Society of the City of New York, the same of which Mrs. Richey Levy was a directress at the time of her death, and of which Mistress I. B. Kursheedt was first Directress in 1850, Three Thousand Dollars.

36. I give and bequeath to the Female Hebrew Benevolent (Society) of Philadelphia (Miss Gratz Secretary) Three Thousand Dollars.

37. I give and bequeath to the Hebrew Education Society of Philadelphia (Pennsylvania) Twenty Thousand Dollars.

38. I give to the United Hebrew Benevolent Society of Philadelphia afore-said Three Thousand Dollars.

39. I give and bequeath to the Hebrew Congregation Ashabat Israel of Fells Point Baltimore, Three Thousand Dollars.

40. I give and bequeath to the Hebrew Congregation Beth Shalome of Richmond Virginia, Five Thousand Dollars.

41. I give and bequeath to the Hebrew Congregation Sheareth Israel of Charleston South Carolina the sum of Five Thousand Dollars.

42. I give and bequeath to the Hebrew Congregation Shangarai Shamoyen of Mobile Alabama Two Thousand Dollars.

43. I give and bequeath to the Hebrew Congregation Mikve Israel of Savannah Georgia Five Thousand Dollars.

44. I give and bequeath to the Hebrew Congregation of Montgomery Alabama Two Thousand dollars say ($2000).

45. I give and bequeath to the Hebrew Congregation of Memphis Ten-nesses Two Thousand dollars.

46. I give and bequeath to the Hebrew Congregation Adas Israel of Louisville Kentucky Three Thousand Dollars.

47. I give and bequeath to the Hebrew Congregation Briai Israel (sic) of Cincinnati Ohio Three Thousand Dollars.

48. I tive and bequeath to the Hebrew School Talmud Jeladin of Cin-cinnati Ohio Five Thousand Dollars.

49. I give and bequeath to the Jews Hospital of Cincinnati Ohio Five Thousand Dollars.

50. I give and bequeath to the Hebrew Congregation Tifareth Israel of Cleveland Ohio Three Thousand Dollars.

51. I give and bequeath to the Hebrew Congregation Briai El (sic) of St. Louis Missouri Three Thousand Dollars.

52. I give and bequeath to the Hebrew Congregation of Beth El of Buf-falo New York Three Thousand dollars (say Three Thousand Dollars.)

53. I give and bequeath to the Hebrew Congregation of Beth El of Albany New York Three Thousand Dollars.

54. I give and bequeath to the three following Institutions named in the Will of my greatly beloved brother the late Abraham Touro of Boston, the following Sums.

First, To the Asylum for Orphan Boys in Boston Massachusetts Five Thousand dollars.

Second, To the Female Orphan Asylum of Boston aforesaid, Five Thou-sand Dollars.

Third, And to the Massachusetts General Hospital Ten Thousand Dollars.

55. I give and bequeath Ten Thousand dollars for the purpose of paying the salary of a Reader or Minister to officiate at the Jewish Synagogue of New Port Rhode Island and to endow the Ministry of the same as well as to keep in repair and embellish the Jewish Cemetary (sic) of New Port afore-said; the said amount to be appropriated and paid or invested for that purpose in such manner, as my Executors may determine Concurrently with the

Corporation of New Port aforesaid, if necessary; And it is my wish and desire that David Gould and Nathan H. Gould sons of my Esteemed friend the late Isaac Gould Esq of New Port aforesaid, should continue to oversee the Improvements in said Cemetary and direct the same, and as a testimony of my regards and in consideration of Services rendered by their Said Father, I give and bequeath the Sum of Two Thousand Dollars to be equally divided between them, the said David and said Nathan H. Gould.

56. I give and bequeath Five Thousand Dollars to Miss Catherine Hays now of Richmond Virginia, as an expression of the Kind remembrance in which that esteemed friend is held by me.

57. I give and bequeath to the Misses Catherine, Harriet and Julia Myers, the three daughters of Mr. Moses M. Myers of Richmond Virginia the Sum of Seven Thousand Dollars to be equally divided between them.

58. I give and bequeath the Sum of Seven Thousand Dollars to the Surviving Children of the late Samuel Myers of Richmond Virginia, to be equally divided between them in token of my remembrance.

59. I give and bequeath to my Friend Mr. Supply Clapp Thwing of Boston Massachusetts, the sum of Five Thousand Dollars as a token of my esteem and Kind remembrance.

60. I give and bequeath the sum of Three Thousand Dollars to my respected friend the Rev. Isaac Leeser of Philadelphia as a token of my regard.

61. I give and bequeath the Sum of Three Thousand Dollars to my friends the Rev. Moses N. Nathan, now of London and his wife to be equally divided between them.

62. I give and bequeath the Sum of Three Thousand dollars to my friend the Rev. Theodore Clapp of New Orleans, in token of my remembrance.

63. To Mistress Ellen Brooks, the Wife of Gorham Brooks Esquire of Boston Massachusetts and daughter of my friend & Executor Rezin Davis Shepherd, I give the sum of Five Thousand dollars, the same to be employed by my Executor in the purchase of a suitable Memorial to be presented to her as an earnest of my very Kind regard.

64. I give and bequeath the sum of Twenty Five Hundred dollars to be employed by my executors in the purchase of a suitable Memorial of my esteem to be presented to Mrs. M. D. Josephs wife of my friend Aaron K. Josephs of this City.

65. I give and bequeath the Sum of Twenty Five Hundred dollars to be employed by my Executors in the purchase of a suitable Memorial of my esteem for Mistress Rebecca Kursheedt wife of Mr. Benjamin Florance of New Orleans.

66. I revoke all other Wills or Testaments which I may have made previously to these presents.

Thus it was that this Testament or last Will was dictated to me, the notary, by the said Testator in presence of the witnesses herein-above named and undersigned and I have written the same such as it was dictated to me, by the Testator, in my own proper hand in presence of Said Witnesses: and having read this Testament in a loud and audible voice to the said Testator, in presence of Said Witnesses, he, the Said Testator, declared in the same presence that he well understood the Same and persisted therein.

All of which was done at one time, without interruption or turning aside to other acts.

Thus Done and passed at the said City of New Orleans at the Said residence of the said Mr. Judah Touro, the day, month and year first before written in the presence of Messieurs Jonathan Montgomery, Henry Shepherd Jr. and George Washington Lee, all three being the Witnesses as aforesaid, who with the Said Testator, and me, the Said Notary have hereunto signed their names.

"Signed" J. Touro--J. Montgomery--Henry Shepherd--Geo. W. Lee --Thos Layton, Not: Pub:

I Certify the foregoing to be a true copy of the original act, on file of Record in my office.

In faith whereof I grant these presents, under my signature, and the impress of my Seal of office, at the City of New Orleans, this Twenty First day of January 1854.

Signed

Thos Layton Not: Pub:

"WE ARE LOOKED UPON AS TRANSITORY INHABITANTS"
1855

> This message was addressed to American Jews urging that
> at least a number of them turn to the land and become farm-
> ers in America.

Sir!

The necessity to direct the attention of the Israelites of America to agriculture has long been felt. The exclusive pursuit of commerce and its cognate branches by our people, is often used as a reproach and it must be con-
fessed with some good show of reason. The mechanical arts have found few
representatives amongst us in this country, a few trades having been entirely monopolized, whilst many of the more elevated, requiring higher
manual skill and technical perfection are in vain sought for. The agriculturist however is entirely wanting. It is on this account that we are looked
upon as transitory inhabitants, having neither the desire nor the capacity
to settle as permanent citizens.

This view erroneous in itself is nevertheless justified by the exclusive
pursuit of commerce, which permits the accumulation of wealth without the
acquirement of permanent interest in the soil of the land which constitutes
the real title to citizenship and to the full enjoyment of civic rights.

In a sound national economy, in which all are benefited by one and one
by all, an undue preponderance of any particular interest, must work in-
juriously upon the wellfare (sic) of the whole. If then, we as a Jewish community push exclusively the commercial interest, it is clear we pursue a
course inimical to the wellfare (sic) of our country.

In order then to change this undesirable state of affairs, in order to
create a taste for and encourage agriculture amongst our people, a calling
so honorable and ensuring the greatest degree of independance (sic) and
happiness and finally in order to employ the newly arrived emigrants, and
the working man generally in want of employment and to give them a chance
to gain by honesty and industry a comparatively happy living and to wean them
from beggary and from becoming a burden to our charitable institutions, it
is proposed to organize an association under the title "American Hebrew
Agricultural and Horticultural Association" to be chartered under the general act of the legislature of the state of New York, passed April 1848, and
governed according to a constitution, to be accepted by the society in proper
time, best calculated to ensure the desired object.

It is proposed to have the society consist of share holders, of an indef-
inite number, each share to the amount of $12, one Dollar to be paid in
monthly.

As soon as circumstances will permit the Association will purchase a tract of land. If said land can be purchased in the neighborhood of New York it would be advisable to turn first to Horticulture, Botanic, i.e. the raising of vegetables, of flowers, to the culture of wool and silk, the raising &c. of cattle poultry, the making of cheese and butter and so forth, because these branches pay better within the reach of this metropolis, and will form a more agreeable transition from other trades to that of agriculture.

There shall be a competent and reliable manager to superintend the whole property of the Association, who shall give ample security and into whose hands is to be confided the management of the soil, the division of labour, but being bound to give strict account of every transaction.

A person applying to be sent there must be of proper age and of good character. He shall receive all the necessaries of life in consideration of his diligent and honest labour. He shall be well treated, used according to his capacities, and instructed in Horticulture and Agriculture theoretically and practically. If his labours are more worth than his board and keeping, a due credit shall be given him monthly and said surplus paid in as shares, at the usual rate of $12 per share. He will thus become materially interested in the soil upon which he works.

The yearly net profits shall be laid out in Dividents (sic) and every share receive an equal amount of said Dividend, which it is supposed will more than tripple (sic) the original sum invested.

A certain sum, shall be applied annually to the building of new houses, schools, houses of worship and learning, to the purchase of cattle, seed, implements and general improvements, so as to enlarge from year to year the sphere of action and usefulness of the Association.

Thus it will be possible to establish as it were a school for those desirous to turn agriculturist, it will create a taste for it in those whom poverty and want of employment has driven there. It will repay the outlays of the shareholders and be an honour to us and a great benefit to our country.

We submit this outline to you, relying upon your hearty co-operation. We have the liveliest conviction that the plan is good and practicable and that it wants only for its fullest realization a generous support, a decided, hearty good will, "a pull, a strong pull and a pull together."

You are therefore respectfully invited to attend a mass meeting where this subject will be considered, on the 13th inst. 8 o'clock P.M. at No. 56 Orchard str. in the room of the Maimonides Library Association where several distinguished speakers are invited to address the meeting.

Respectfully yours

B. Rothshild, J. Rosenbourgh, Dr. S. Waterman, Henry American, Maurice Werner, Samuel Trechet, Gottlieb, Rosenblatt, H. Hindburghauser, S. Kimmelstiel, A. Asch, E. Buchstein, S. Engel, Hyman Gutman, J. Sulzberger, S. Straus, Ch. Northschild, H. Straus, Henry Kling, J. Muhlhauser, A. Chailly.

"BEING OF JEWISH PERSUASION"
1857

While he is today regarded as a hero by the United States
Navy, Captain Uriah P. Levy faced considerable ostracism,
insult, and as many as six court martials, because of his
Jewish faith. In 1855 he was dismissed "to improve the efficiency of the navy." Public protest brought about a Court
of Inquiry and it is the defense Levy made before this court
which follows. He was reinstated in 1858 and ended his naval career as the commander of the Mediterranean squadron.

...My parents were Israelites, and I was nurtured in the faith of my
ancestors. In deciding to adhere to it, I have but exercised a right, guar-
anteed to me by the constitution of my native State, and of the United States
--a right given to all men by their Maker--a right more precious to each
of us than life itself. But, while claiming and exercising this freedom of
conscience, I have never failed to acknowledge and respect the like freedom
of others. I might safely defy the citation of a single act, in the whole
course of my official career, injurious to the religious rights of any other
person. Remembering always that the great mass of my fellow-citizens
were Christians; profoundly grateful to the Christian founders of our republic, for their justice and liberality to my long persecuted race; I have earnestly endeavored, in all places and circumstances, to act up to the wise
and tolerant spirit of our political institutions. I have therefore been care-
ful to treat every Christian, and especially every Christian under my command, with exemplary justice and ungrudging liberality. Of this, you have
had clear proof so far as my command of the Vandalia is concerned, from
the lips of Lieutenants (Edmund) Lanier and (John N.) Maffit. They testify
to the observance, on board that ship, under the standing rules and regulations prescribed by me, of the Christian Sabbath, and to the scrupulous
regard paid by me on all occasions, to the religious rights and feelings of
the officers and men.
    I have to complain--more in sorrow than in anger do I say it--that in
my official experience I have met with little to encourage, though with much
to frustrate, these conciliatory efforts. At an early day, and especially
from the time when it became known to the officers of my age and grade,
that I aspired to a lieutenancy, and still more, after I had gained it, I was
forced to encounter a large share of the prejudice and hostility by which,
for so many ages, the Jew has been pursued. I need not speak to you of the
incompatibility of these sentiments with the genius of Christianity, or the
precepts of its author. You should know this far better than I; but I may
ask you to unite with the wisest and best men of our own country and of
Europe, in denouncing them, not merely as injurious to the peace and

welfare of the community, but as repugnant to every dictate of reason, humanity and justice.

In February, 1818, I was transferred, by Commodore (Charles) Stewart, from his ship, the Franklin, 74, to the frigate United States, under the command of Captain (William M.) Crane. Under the influence of the double projudice to which I have alluded, a conspiracy was formed among certain officers of this frigate to prevent my reception in her. Commodore (T.A.C.) Jones, in answer to the eighth interrogatory on my part, gives a full account of it. He says:

"Lieutenant Levy, for several months, was fourth, and I first lieutenant, of the frigate United States, where he discharged his duty satisfactorily to the captain as well as to the first lieutenant, notwithstanding his advent into our ship was attended with such novel and discouraging circumstances as, in justice to captain Levy, renders it necessary here to record them.

"On the arrival of the Franklin, of 74 guns, at Syracuse, in 1818, bearing the broad pennant of commodore Charles Stewart, to relieve commodore (John S.) Chauncey, then in command of the Mediterranean squadron, it was understood that lieutanant Levy, a supernumerary on board of the Franklin, was to be ordered to the frigate United States, then short of her complement of lieutenants. Whereupon, the ward-room mess, without consulting me, determined to remonstrate against Levy's coming aboard. I was called on by a member of the mess to communicate their wishes to Captain Crane and ask his interference.

"Astonished at such a proposition, I inquired as to the cause, when I was answered, that he was a Jew, and not an agreeable person, and they did not want to be brought in contact with him in our then very pleasant and harmonious mess of some eight or nine persons; and, moreover, that he was an interloper, having entered the navy as master, to the prejudice of the older midshipmen, &c. &c. Such was the reply, in substance, to my inquiry. I then asked the relator if he, or any member of our mess, knew anything of his own knowledge, derogatory to lieutenant Levy, as an officer and as a gentleman. The answer was no, but they had heard thus and so, &c., &c. I endeavored to point out the difficulties that might result from a procedure so much at variance with military subordination, and the justice due to a brother officer, against whom they had nothing but vague and ill-defined rumors; but my counsel then did not prevail. The remonstrance was made directly to captain Crane, and by captain Crane to Commodore Stewart. Levy soon after reported on board the frigate United States, for duty. When Lieutenant Levy came on board, he asked a private interview with me, wishing my advice as the procedures he ought to pursue under such embarrassing circumstances. I gave it freely and simply, to the effect, vis.: do your duty as an officer and a gentleman, be civil to all, however reserved you may choose to be to any, and the first man who observed a different course towards you, call him to a strict and prompt account. Our messmates were gentlemen, and having perceived their error before lieutenant Levy got on board, had, in accordance with my previous advice, determined to receive lieutenant Levy as a gentleman and a brother officer, and to respect and treat him as such, till by his conduct he should prove himself unworthy. I continued a few months longer on board the frigate United States, as her first lieutenant, during the whole of which time Lieutenant Levy's conduct and deportment was altogether unexceptionable, and I know that, perhaps with a single exception, those who opposed his joining our mess, not only relented, but deeply regretted the false step they had incautiously taken. "

During the few months that Commodore Jones remained in the ship United States, his wise and just counsels had the effect he describes. After he left her, I am sorry to be obliged to say, the old prejudices revived in the breasts of too many of my associates.

In December, 1824, a conspiracy of the same kind was formed among the junior officers of the ward-room mess, on board the North Carolina. She was about to sail for the Mediterranean to join the squadron in that sea; and I was ordered to take passage in her, and to report myself to Commodore Creighton, the commander-in-chief of the squadron. Commodore Isaac Mayo, one of the witnesses produced by me, gives a full account of this cabal, and of his refusal to join it. His testimony will be referred to hereafter, in another connexion....

In 1844, the President (John Tyler) nominated me to the Senate for promotion as a captain. This nomination was confirmed on the (31st) day of May, 1844, --my appointment to take rank from the 29th March, 1844. The circumstances attending this appointment were of peculiar interest to me; and it is most important that they should be fully understood by the Court. Attempts were made, outside the Senate, by certain officers of the Navy, to induce that body to reject my nomination. The naval Committee of the Senate, to whom the nomination had been referred, were approached by officers hostile to or prejudiced against me; and such objections were made to my appointment, that the committee felt it proper to call on the Secretary of the Navy for all papers on file relating to my official conduct. The archives of the Department were ransacked; charges preferred against me during my service as sailing-master, lieutenant and commander, growing (with a single exception) out of those petty altercations and personal quarrels unfortunately too common in our profession, were raked up; and the records of all the courts martial before which, in the course of thirty years, I had been brought, were laid before the committee. These documents having been thoroughly examined by them, they reported in favor of the nomination; and on their report it was unanimously confirmed.

When, in 1855, I complained to the Secretary (of the Navy, James C.) Dobbin of "some unseen influence" seeking "through unmerited prejudice to injure me with the Department, " and to prevent it from according to me my just rights, I stated that I then fully believed, and what I had long before suspected to be the fact, I was driven to this conclusion by the persistent refusal of the several secretaries to employ me, in the face of all the proofs of my fitness, in the records of the Department, and of the recommendations and support of so many distinguished men, in support of my applications. I could draw, from the circumstances, no other inference; nor do I think that any other can be drawn by you. But the fact is not now left to inference merely. You have, in the deposition of the Secretary, Mr. (George) Bancroft, direct evidence of the fact. In answer to the ninth interrogatory on my part, he says:

"When Secretary of the Navy, I never had cause to doubt, and never doubted, Captain Levy's competence to serve the United States in the grade of captain. I did not find myself able to give him a command, for three reasons:

1st. The excessive number of officers of his grade made it impossible to employ all of them who were fit.

2d. The good of the service, moreover, seemed to require bringing forward officers less advanced in years than most of the captains, and the law sanctioned that course.

3d. I perceived a strong prejudice in the service against Captain Levy, which seemed to me, in a considerable part, attributable to his being of the Jewish persuasion; and while I, as an executive officer, had the same liberal views which guided the President and Senate in commissioning him as a captain, I always endeavored in fitting out ships to have some reference to that harmonious co-operation which is essential to the highest effectiveness.

To the first of these reasons no exception can be taken. The second is founded on a favorite theory of Mr. Bancroft, while Secretary, to which, were it impartially carried out, I should be as little disposed to object as any other officer of my rank and age.

The third reason assigned by Mr. Bancroft, though last in order, is not least in importance.

The fact that it is assigned by him as one of the reasons for not giving me a command, justified the inference that the first two reasons would not have been sufficient to produce that result without the addition of the third.

From what source and in what manner, Mr. Bancroft perceived the strong prejudice in the service against me, of which he speaks, he does not state. But it is easy to trace it to its origin. He had never been officially connected with the Navy until he came to Washington in 1845, as head of the Department. He was then brought into intercourse with such officers of the Navy as were enabled, by their rank, their connection with bureaux, or their social position, to cultivate the acquaintance, and get the ear of the secretary. It was only by means of such intercourse, that it was possible for him to become acquainted with the prejudices which existed in the service against any of its members. It was only in this way that he could learn that any such prejudice existed against me. Among the officers of the Navy to whom the secretary was thus peculiarly accessible, there were some who were friendly to me; but there were others who were not only unfriendly, but also active and bitter in their hostility against me. How else than through intercourse with those who had the motive, and took the pains, to force it upon him, was it possible for Mr. Bancroft to know that any prejudice existed against me in the Navy; and how could he form any estimate as to its strength, except from the frequency and rancour with which it was obtruded upon his notice?

From the same source which informed him of the prejudice, he learned its nature and grounds--the chief, if not the sole ground, being my peculiar religious faith--my "being of the Jewish persuasion." Doubtless, those who could make such a fact the pretext for a prejudice against a brother officer, so inveterate and unyielding, as to compel the head of the department reluctantly to recognise and admit as--to some extent at least--an element of his official action, would not scruple to disparage and traduce, in other respects, the object of their aversion. But even their efforts failed to awaken, for a moment, in the mind of the secretary, a solitary doubt as to my competence. This he tells us in the most emphatic terms.

In the satisfaction which this avowal gives me--in the gratitude I owe, and shall ever cherish, to one who, in spite of such efforts, retained towards me an opinion so favorable--I could almost pass over, without remark, the injury done me--most unwittingly, I am sure--by his allowing to such an objection any weight whatever. Had it then come to my knowledge, I could have shown him, just as I have now shown to you, from the records of the department, that during my year's command of the Vandalia, my religious faith never impaired the efficiency of my ship; that I never permitted it to interfere with the rights, or to wound the feelings, of my Christian officers and men; and that I did what I could, and all that they desired, to respect and satisfy those rights and feelings. I might have shown to him, as I have shown to you, by the evidence of the many officers, who, in this investigation, have testified in my behalf, that the prejudice to which he was constrained to give such serious effect against me, was far from being so general or so strong as he was led to believe;--that officers, more in number than my draducers, and far better qualified to judge, were untainted by it --treated it with contempt, and denounced it as inconsistent with the spirit of our institutions--unworthy of the present age, and degrading to the honor of the naval service. And I might thus, perhaps, have afforded him the opportunity, which, I doubt not, he would gladly have seized, not only from a sense of justice to myself, but in accordance with his own liberal and enlightened convictions, of setting his face, like a flint, against the double-headed hydra of personal prejudice and religious bigotry, and of driving it forever from the councils of his department. The benefit of such an act to myself would have been insignificant, in comparison with the vindication it would have furnished of the dignity and justice of our Government, and its faithful conservation of the most sacred of our public and private rights....

Mr. President and Gentlemen of the Court:

My defence, so far as it depends on the examination of the evidence, is before you; and here, perhaps, I ought to stop. But the peculiarities of my case--the importance and far-reaching interest of the principles it involves --requires, what I hope you will allow me, a few additional remarks.

That the allegation of unfitness for the naval service, made against me by the Government, was wholly unsupported by evidence; and that I have made out a complete defense against the attempt to justify my dismissal, and an affirmative title to restoration, by the proofs on my part; these I regard as undeniable propositions. And yet there are those connected with the navy, who, notwithstanding all the proofs I have produces, are hostile to my restoration. This, it would be vain to deny to others, or to conceal from myself. Should any one of these dare to obtrude upon you the opinion or the wish, that I should not be restored; or, being restored, should not be placed upon the active list; you have only to refer him to the oath which you have taken, to silence and rebuke him. Permit me--not that I suppose you can have forgotten its terms, but because of their peculiar pertinency to my case--to quote the closing words of this oath. It not only requires you, as before remarked "well and truly to examine and inquire, according to the evidence, into the matter now before you;" but, to do this, "without partiality or prejudice." This oath, although exceedingly brief, is exceedingly comprehensive and precise. The lawmakers who framed it well know the special dangers to which Courts of Inquiry are exposed--partiality towards influential prosecutors and accusers, and prejudice against the accused. Against these, the oath solemnly warns you; and if ever there was a case in which such a warning was right and seasonable, this is that case.

The Government, with its vase power and influence, is, in name at least, my prosecutor. Men in high places, who have once done me grievous wrong, are interested to prevent the remedying of that wrong. There are others, not without their influence, who, by their activity in support of the wrong, and in opposition to the remedy, have a common interest with my prosecutors.

Never, on the other hand, was there a man, in the ranks of our profession, against whom, in the breasts of certain members of that profession, prejudices so unjust and yet so strong, have so long and so incessantly rankled. Such, too, are the origin and character of these prejudices, as to make them, of all others, the most inveterate and unyielding. The prejudice felt by men of little minds, who think themselves, by the accidental circumstances of wealth or ancestry, better than the less favored of their fellows; the prejudice of caste, which looks down on the man who, by honest toil, is the maker of his own fortunes; this prejudice is stubborn as well as bitter, and of this I have had, as you have seen the proofs, my full share. But this is placable and transient compared with that generated and nourished by religious intolerance and bigotry.

The first article of the amendments to the Constitution of the United States, specially declares, in its first clause, that "Congress shall make no law respecting an establishment of religion, or prohibiting the free exercise thereof;" thus showing by its place, no less than by its language, how highly freedom of conscience was valued by the founders of our Republic. In the constitutions of the several States, now in force, the like provision is contained. Our liberality and justice, in this regard, have been honored by the friends of liberty and human rights throughout the world. An eminent British writer, about thirty years ago, in the ablest of their reviews, used, in reference to this point, the following language:

"They have fairly and completely, and probably forever, extinguished that spirit of religious persecution which has been the employment and the curse of mankind, for four or five centuries; not only that persecution which imprisons and scourges for religious opinions, but the tyranny of incapacitation, which by disqualifying from civil offices, and cutting a man off from the lawful objects of ambition, endeavors to strangle religious freedom in silence, and to enjoy all the advantages, without the blood, and noise, and fire of persecution. * * * * * * * * * In this particular, the Americans are at the head of all the nations of the world. *"

Little did the author of this generous tribute to our country suspect, that even while he was penning it, there were those in the American navy, with whom it was a question whether a Jew should be tolerated in the service? Still less did he dream, that at the very moment when, in his own country, a representative of the illustrious house of RUSSELL, eminent by his services in the cause of freedom, of education, and of justice, is about giving himself, with the full assent of his government, to the work of Jewish emancipation, a spectacle like the present should be witnessed in this land of equality and freedom. For with those who would now deny to me, because of my religious faith, the restoration, to which, by half a century of witnesses, I have proved myself entitled, what is it but an attempt to place the professors of this faith under the ban of incapacitation?

This is the case before you; and, in this view, its importance cannot be overrated. It is the case of every Israelite in the Union. I need not speak to you of their number. They are unsurpassed by any portion of our people in loyalty to the Constitution and to the Union; in their quiet obedience to the laws; and in the cheerfulness with which they contribute to the public burthens. Many of them have been distinguished by their liberal donations to the general interests of education and of charity; in some cases, too-- of which the name of JUDAH TOURO will remind you--to charities controlled by Christians. And of all my brethren in this land--as well those of foreign birth as of American descent--how rarely does any one of them become a

---

* Sydney Smith, in Edinburgh Review, July, 1824, (p. 429).

charge on your State or municipal treasuries! How largely do they all contribute to the activities of trade; to the interests of commerce; to the stock of public wealth! Are all these to be proscribed? And is this to be done while we retain in our Constitution the language I have quoted? Is this language to be spoken to the ear, but broken to the hope, of my race? Are the thousands of Judah and the ten thousands of Israel, in their dispersions throughout the earth, who look to America, as a land bright with promise --are they now to learn, to their sorrow and dismay, that we, too, have sunk into the mire of religious intolerance and bigotry? And are American Christians now to begin the persecution of the Jews? Of the Jews, who stand among them the representatives of the patriarchs and prophets, --the Jews, to whom were committed the oracles of God, --the Jews, from whom these oracles have been received, and who are the living witnesses of their truth; --the Jews, from whom came the founder of Christianity;--the Jews, to whom, as Christians themselves believe, have been made promises of greatness and of glory, in whose fulfilment are bound up the hopes, not merely of the remnant of Israel, but of all the races of men? And think not, if you once enter on this career, that it can be limited to the Jew.   What is my case to-day, if you yield to this injustice, may to-morrow be that of the Roman Catholic or the Unitarian; the Episcopalian or the Methodist; the Presbyterian or the Baptist.   There is but one safeguard; and this is to be found in an honest, whole-hearted, inflexible support of the wise, the just, the impartial guarantee of the Constitution.   I have the fullest confidence that you will faithfully adhere to this guarantee; and, therefore, with like confidence, I leave my destiny in your hands.

U. P. LEVY.

"OF WHOM THE MAJORITY ARE RATHER INDIGENT"
1860

This editorial appeared in The Journal of Commerce in New York City. While much of it was based upon doubtful if not limited knowledge about the Jews, it is significant as it does reflect an attitude toward Jews by an important part of the non-Jewish business community toward the largest Jewish community in the country.

The Jewish year 5621 has just been ushered in, and we have passed through its opening solemnities. The Hebrews of the metropolis, throwing aside for the moment all worldly cares, join faithfully in the ceremonies peculiar to the people, which have been so perseveringly celebrated and so carefully transmitted through many generations that have lived since the destruction of Jerusalem and the banishment of its inhabitants. Not the least wonderful, even of the many wonderful things of our day, and a living proof of the truth of Christianity, is the distinct and separate preservation, without the least shadow of a national abode, of a people numbering millions of individuals, scattered throughout every division and district of the world, possessing talent sufficient, not only for self-government, but of science or of art to which they devote themselves, exhibiting a fortitude in suffering and an energy in favorable circumstances that have excited the amazement, if not the admiration of all classes. They mingle continually with the business men of different nations, aid in the formation and support of various governments, render their assistance almost whenever and wherever required, and yet remain completely isolated, maintaining a pride of origin that almost forbids sympathy or pity. In this city, and generally throughout this country, where their rights are never invaded, they live so quietly that unless one goes into their quarters, he seldom meets with them. A few of our citizens know them socially, and all are too willing to believe Shylock their true type. But although, as a whole, the Jews have neglected education, and comparatively few have accepted the means of mental improvement placed within their reach by the governments under which they live, some have stepped forth from the ranks, and braving the Christian prejudices that have been accumulating for ages, have drawn the attention of mankind, and left their names on the page of history. Such instances are not very common, because the Jews, for the most part, are so content to live quietly and unostentatiously, and those who are remarkable for their intellectual powers are so inclined to give their undivided attention to the study of ancient records and commentaries. Still the Jews in Europe frequently make valuable contributions to literature and art, and it is not unusual on the continent to find them holding professorships. Such names as Rothschild, Disraeli, Beethoven, Mendelssohn, and Rachel, illustrate the variety of their talents and the greatness of their capacity, and there is no reason to doubt that, under favorable circumstances, and with such incentives as a fixed national habitation only could furnish, they would develop the same genius that was manifested by their early lawgivers, generals, and historians.

In this city their number, at present, is about 40,000, of whom the majority are rather indigent, and either because they begin the battle of life while very young, or are disinclined to social intercourse with others, (having no distinct literary institutions of their own.) or both, they remain uneducated. Their national studies, even if generally pursued, could not give that knowledge of the sciences without which it is impossible to keep pace with the rapid strides of civilization in our day. The minds of such students may be cultivated, but they are not enlightened.

There are seventeen synagogues in New York. The first was erected in Mill St., now South William St., in 1729, where the congregation worshipped for more than a century. Some twenty-five years ago or more they removed to Crosby St., and recently have dedicated a new synagogue in West Nineteenth St., said to be more imposing in appearance than any other in the United States. It is built of Nova Scotia stone, in a style combining two orders of architecture--the Ionic and Corinthian. The entire cost of the structure and its site, was about $110,000.

This city, also, contains a hospital, supported at the expense of the Jews, and as a proof of liberality really existing among them, for which they are rarely credited, it may be mentioned that two years ago they raised $10,000 as the net proceeds of a ball given to sustain it. Preparations are making to repeat the experiment. Six months ago $20,000 was raised by the Jews of this country, numbering but 150,000, for their brethren in Morocco, who were suffering from the war then raging.

In Philadelphia, 15,000 members have established seven Hebrew congregations, two educational and eleven charitable associations, and a publication society.

The Jews are scattered over the whole country, but are more numerous in commercial cities and towns. Throughout the West, especially, wherever there is a chance for profitable trade, they have insinuated themselves. Two synagogues were recently dedicated in Cincinnati. Wherever they go, their institutions accompany them as invariably as the household gods went with the ancient Romans.

Since the commencement of the present month, the Jews in this city have been almost constantly occupied in the observance of various solemnities. The Feast of Tabernacles, the Feast of Palms, and the Feast of the Law, have followed each other in quick succession. In a few weeks they will be called on to observe the Feast of the Dedication of the Temple then a Fast commemorative of the Destruction of Jerusalem. What a world of emotion the celebration of these revered ceremonies must excite! How must the Jew mourn over the departed glories of a nation once so powerful and renowned, now weak and fallen! Is it after all very wonderful that men who can trace their lineage to such an origin, should cling with tenacious vigor to their rites and refuse to blend with others of the race? Is it strange that they wish to preserve pure in their veins the blood of Moses, of David, of Solomon, and the Prophets?

Jerusalem was taken by Titus on the 8th of September, A.D. 70. Ninety-seven thousand prisoners were captured during the siege, and eleven thousand died of starvation. The loss of the Jews in killed, wounded and missing, during the war, is computed in round numbers at 1,400,000. The Emperor Vespasian disposed of the Jewish lands for his own use, compelled the conquered people to pay into his treasury the usual tribute of the sanctuary, and cut off the branches of the House of Judah that he might forever deprive them of the hope of deliverance from a coming Messiah. Broken hearted, they left the land they loved so well, never since to return. They have wandered over Africa and settled on its Eastern and Northern coasts, have traveled far into Asia, within the walls of China, have sought the frozen regions of Russia, the beautiful lands of Spain and Italy, and the wild mountains of Switzerland, have taken up their abode in Germany and Holland, in France, England, Sweden, Norway--in fact, in every land under the sun, --everywhere abused and persecuted with a severity and malignity that know no parallel in history. During the past century, however, one government after another has made concessions in their favor, and under this milder treatment they have rapidly increased in numbers and in influence. Even Russia has acknowledged their importance as citizens, and 2,000,000 of them dwell within her empire. In Germany they are very numerous; the chief magistrate of Hamburg is a Jew. Poland is their stronghold; within its former limits 1,000,000 of them may be counted. Nearly half a million are in Morocco; 90,000 in Constantinople; 70,000 in Italy; 40,000 in England. The whole number on the globe is variously estimated at from 6,000,000 to 12,000,000: the probable number is 8,000,000. Of course, no pretensions to accuracy can be made in such a computation: there are tribes said to be running wild in the interior of Africa.

A movement has been initiated at Paris, with the knowledge, and possibly at the instance of the Emperor Napoleon, for the purpose of organizing the whole people into associations, and establishing communication among them. They have long cherished the expectation of return to the Holy Land. May some of them not think that their restoration draws near? The signs of the times encourage the hope. The Turkish Empire is falling in pieces, and the occupation of the ancient Canaan by an essentially trading people, when the Suez canal shall have been opened, will add to the commercial facilities and wealth of the world. It is said that Baron Rothschild is intimate with the Emperor, and, ambitions to distinguish himself in the service of his nation, keeps the project constantly before him.

"WE...SCORN AND REPEL YOUR ADVICE..."
1861

This resolution of the Hebrew Congregation of Shreveport, Louisiana, reflects a perhaps minority view held by Jews in the South concerning the raging conflict between the Union and the Confederacy, but still a view held by more than one Jewish community in Dixie. The resolution itself was in response to an editorial appeal of the popular Jewish periodical, The Jewish Messenger, for support of the Union cause.

Whereas, we received the "Jewish Messenger" on the 26th of April, a paper published in New York, in which an appeal has been made to all, whether native or foreign born, Christian or Israelite. An article headed "stand by the Flag!" in which the editor makes an appeal to support the stars and stripes, and to rally as one man for the Union and the Constitution. Therefore be it.

Resolved, That we, the Hebrew congregation of Shreveport, scorn and repel your advice, although we might be called Sourthern rebels; still, as law-abiding citizens, we solemnly pledge ourselves to stand by, protect, and honor the flag, with its stars and stripes, the Union and Constitution of the Southern Confederacy with our lives, liberty, and all that is dear to us.

Resolved, That we, the members of said congregation, bind ourselves to discontinue the subscription of the "Jewish Messenger," and all Northern papers opposed to our holy cause, and also to use all honorable means in having said paper banished from our beloved country.

Resolved, That while we mistook your paper for a religious one, which ought to be strictly neutral in politics, we shall from this out treat it with scorn, as a black republican paper, and not worthy of Southern patronage; and that, according to our understanding, church and politics ought never to be mingled, as it has been the ruination of any country captivated by the enticing words of preachers.

Resolved, That we, the members of said congregation, have lost all confidence and regard to the Rev. S.M. Isaacs, Editor and Proprietor of the "Jewish Messenger," and see in him an enemy to our interest and welfare, and believe it to be more unjust for one who preaches the Word of God, and to advise us to act as traitors and renegades to our adopted country, and raise hatred and dissatisfaction in our midst, and assisting to start a bloody civil war amongst us.

Resolved, That we believe like the Druids of old, the duties of those who preach the Holy Word to be first in the line of battle, and to cheer up those fighting for liberty against their oppressors, in place of those who are proclaiming now from their pulpits, words to encourage an excited people, and praying for bloody vengence against us. Brutus, while kissing Caesar, plunged the dagger to his heart.

 <u>Resolved,</u> That a copy of these resolutions be sent to the editor of the "Jewish Messenger".

 <u>Resolved,</u> That papers friendly to the Southern cause, are politely requested to publish the foregoing resolutions.

M. Bauer, <u>President</u>

Ed. Eberstadt, Secretary, <u>pro tem.</u>

"AND WITH NO OTHER PROOF THAN THAT THEY WERE MEMBERS OF A CERTAIN RELIGIOUS DENOMINATION" 1863

On November 9 and 10, 1862, Major-General U.S. Grant who was in command of the Department of the Tennessee, which included northern Mississippi and parts of Kentucky and Tennessee west of the Tennessee River, issued orders to officers in Jackson, Tenn., forbidding travel south of Jackson to all persons, "the Israelites especially," because they were "such an intolerable nuisance." This was a reference to the speculators who had swarmed into the area to exploit the rising cotton market. Some of these speculators were Jewish, but Grant identified the whole traffic with the Jews and issued Order No. 11 which was a clearly discriminatory action. This is a newspaper account of the order and its revocation by President Lincoln which was written by Rabbi Isaac Mayer Wise who was a member of a delegation sent to meet with Lincoln on the matter.

Washington, D.C., Jan. 8. (1863)

The history of General Grant's order and its revocation forms quite an interesting chapter in the annals of the day. Gentlemen from Paducah, Ky., telegraphed to the President, who informed General Halleck instantly; we wrote immediately to Secretary (of War) Stanton; but neither the former nor the latter believed that Gen. Grant could have issued an order so absurd and ridiculous, and, therefore, did not do anything in the matter. When Mr. Kaskel came to Washington, January 3, and was introduced to the President, by Mr. Gurley of Cincinnati, the President at once gave order to Gen. Halleck to revoke said order. General Halleck would not believe in the existence of such order, till Mr. Kaskel showed him the official copy. General Halleck instantly and peremptorily revoked the order and telegraphed to Gen. Grant to inform all post commanders instantly, of the will of the government in this matter. The Cincinnati and Louisville delegation came too late. --The order was rescinded. Still we thought it proper to see the President and express our thanks for his promptness in this matter. --Mark, however, how democratic things look in Washington. We arrived from Baltimore about 5 P.M. on Wednesday (January 6), arrived in the hotel without changing clothes. Rev. Dr. Lilienthal inquired and was informed that Mr. Gurley was in the same house, but was not in at present. Meanwhile, Mr. Bijur and myself went to Mr. Pendleton of Cincinnati and talked half an hour to him.

On returning to our hotel we met Mr. Gurley, who without bestowing any consideration on our traveling garbs, went with us to the White House and before 8 P.M. we were introduced to the President, who being all alone, received us with that frank cordiality, which, though usually neglected, becomes men high in office so well. Having expressed our thanks for the promptness and dispatch in revoking Gen. Grant's order, the President gave utterance to his surprise that Gen. Grant should have issued so ridiculous an order, and added--"to condemn a class is, to say the least, to wrong the good with the bad. I do not like to hear a class or nationality condemned on account of a few sinners." The President, we must confess, fully illustrated to us and convinced us that he knows of no distinction between Jew and Gentile, that he feels no prejudice against any nationality, and that he by no means will allow that a citizen in any wise be wronged on account of his place of birth or religious confession. He illustrated this point to us in a very happy manner, of which we can only give the substance at present, and promise to give particulars on another occasion. Now then, in our traveling habiliments, we spoke about half an hour to the President of the U.S. in an open and frank manner, and were dismissed in the same simple style.

Sorry we are to say that Congress did not think proper to be as just as the President is. Congress is not now the people's legislative body, it belongs to a party. Senator Powel(1) of Kentucky, as noted elsewhere, introduced a resolution condemning the unjust order of Gen. Grant, to inform others that orders of this kind must not be issued; but the resolution was tabled to be killed, when called up again. Mr. Pendleton of Cincinnati, attempted in vain on Monday and Tuesday to bring the following resolution before the House. He finally succeeded on Wednesday (yesterday) to propose the following:

Mr. Pendleton offered a preamble setting forth that Major-General Grant, on the 17th of December, as the commander of the Department of the Tennessee, did issue an order stating that the Jews, as a class, had violated every regulation of trade established in that department, and for this were to be expelled from the department within twenty-four hours, &c., and as in the pursuance of the order General Grant caused many peaceful citizens to be expelled within twenty-four hours without allegation of misconduct, and with no other proof than that they were members of a certain religious denomination; and whereas said sweeping order makes no discrimination between the innocent and the guilty, and it is illegal, unjust, tyrannical and cruel, therefore

Resolved, That the said order deserves the sternest condemnation of the House and of the President of the United States as Commander-in-Chief of the Army and Navy.

Mr. PENDLETON moved the previous question on the passage of this proposition.

Mr. WASHBURNE (R) moved that it be laid upon the table; and this was agreed to--yeas 56, nays 53.

On motion of Mr. Washburne, the everlasting Mr. Washburne, the resolution was tabled by a vote of 56 yeas to 53 nays. If the Hebrew citizens of the United States were "gentlemen of color, " Mr. Washburne would certainly have made a brilliant effort to vindicate their rights and expose a general who committed a gross outrage on them. But being only white men, it would not pay. Partisan legislation, that is all we have to expect of this congress. Mr. Pendleton said Washburne's motive was that of friendship for Grant, whom to defend in congress he had several times taken upon himself; but Republican members openly say, it is a rule of the House to vote down every thing coming from the other side, viz: the democratic. How do you like this remarkable impartiality?

Having to see a good many things to-day, we must conclude this, to say more to-morrow.

THE EDITOR.

(Isaac Mayer Wise)

"AMONG THEM ARE SOME OF OUR BEST FRIENDS"
1867

Discrimination against Jewish merchants by insurance companies became a public issue in the 1860's. Suffering heavy losses during the depression years of this period, the insurance companies attempted to reduce risks by ordering their agents to refuse to insure Jews or to insure them only under special circumstances. An editorial in a Philadelphia newspaper dealing with the situation follows.

For some time past the Jews have been very much excited on account of the action of certain insurance companies, who decline to take risks from individuals of that religious belief. Much indignation has been expressed, not only among the Jews, but among citizens of all classes, and the illiberal conduct of the companies has generally been condemned by the better class of business men. The difficulty was first started by the Underwriters' Agency of New York city, an organization representing the Niagara, Republic, Hanover and Germania companies. The agents of this association were instructed to refuse making any insurance on property belonging to Jews. Other companies followed the lead of the Underwriters' Agency; and the Jewish merchants, very properly considering the matter not merely an insult to their religion, but as a reflection of the most serious kind on their integrity as business men, held a meeting to take some action in regard to it. A committee was appointed to consult with the insurance companies, and a circular was issued asking each of them whether they approved of the proscriptive movement. To this a large number of replies were received, all of them written in respectful terms except those from the Home and Metropolitan companies. Others did not reply, and it was consequently concluded that they endorsed the action of the Underwriters' Agency. The committee who had the matter in charge recently made a report to a large meeting of Jewish merchants, who assembled in the synagogue on Nineteenth Street in New York, and they offered the following preamble and resolutions, which were unanimously adopted:

WHEREAS, Unjust discriminations have been adopted by certain insurance companies between citizens professing the Jewish religion and those of other denominations:

And whereas, This course is calculated to deepen prejudices unworthy of the age and country; therefore

Resolved, That duty and self-respect alike demand that we, as Israelites, should cease all connection with such institutions.

Resolved, That the following insurance companies--the Merchants', Croton, Exchange, Firemen's, American Exchange, Howard, National, St. Nicholas, International, Humboldt, Indemnity, Lafayette, Arctic,

Commercial, Corn Exchange, Commerce, Fulton, New Amsterdam, United States, Montauk (of Brooklyn), Jersey City, Enterprise, Firemen's Trust, Peter Cooper, Washington and North River Companies--having failed to reply to the circular of the committee, they recommend that until satisfactory replies are received, our co-religionists do not insure in either of those companies.

Resolved, That the Jewish citizens throughout the United States be requested not to insure in the Home or Metropolitan Companies until the insulting letters sent to the committee be retracted; and finally,

Resolved, That the proceedings of the meeting be published in pamphlet form for distribution throughout the United States.

The Jews say that the dishonesty of one or two persons, even if proved, is no reason why the whole body of Hebrew citizens should be proscribed, and they denounce the action of these insurance companies as nothing more nor less than an attempt at persecution, and as utterly unworthy of the present age and country. It is an undeniable fact that in their business relations the Jews stand as high as any other class in the community. They have a proverbial reputation for close dealing, but the generality of Christian merchants are fully as ready to drive a hard bargain whenever they have an opportunity as any of their Hebrew neighbors. There is this much to be said, however, that when the Jews do conclude a bargain they almost invariably stick to it, and when they undertake to do a thing they seldom fail to carry it out.

During the past nineteen years we have had numerous dealings with Jews, and they have uniformly been of the most satisfactory character. Among them are some of our best friends, and we can bear testimony to their general good conduct as citizens, to their integrity as merchants, to their liberality in religious sentiment, and to their general refinement and intelligence. In all of these respects they are fully the peers of any other religious sect in the country. We seldom or never hear of the failure of a Jewish merchant; Jews are very rarely accused or convicted of crimes, and the community is not charged with the support of Hebrew vagabonds and paupers in our almshouses and prisons. All of these facts speak very highly for the Jews, and show them to be orderly and well-behaved citizens. Besides this they are an unusually well-read and intelligent people, and it is a well known fact that they have among them some of the most learned men of the day. Several years ago there was published in the columns of the Dispatch a "Post-Biblical History of the Jews, " by the celebrated Rabbi Raphael (Raphall) of New York. This work was afterward issued in book form, and was commented upon in favorable terms by the press generally. The London Athenaeum--a journal well qualified to speak in the matter-- pronounced it the best work of the kind ever written.

The peculiarities of the Hebrew religion have a tendency to keep those who adhere to its ancient forms in a measure separated from other citizens, and many persons who have but little to do with them know nothing about their good or bad qualities, and consequently would be likely to take this unjust action of the insurance companies as indicative of a general untrustworthiness on the part of all classes of Jews. Those who are best acquainted with them, and who have had most frequent dealing with them, know that the implied charge against their character is without the slightest foundation.

The Jews are numerous and wealthy enough to organize insurance companies among themselves, and they could readily dispense with assistance of that kind from outsiders; but it it contrary to the interests of the country and to the proper business spirit that any such course should be adopted. The tendency to clannishness among persons of particular nationalities or religious beliefs should be discouraged as inimical to our republican institutions. That such conduct as that of the insurance companies will have the effect to draw the line between the Jewish and Christian religious sects broader and more distinct than it has ever been before must be evident to every one, and the Jews would not certainly be to blame if they were to retaliate by refusing to patronize any insurance companies in which the stock is not held by themselves. We hope that the good sense of our merchants will cause them to look at this matter in the proper light, and to condemn in the strongest terms the insulting action of a portion of the New York insurance companies. If the principle that any set of men are to be proscribed because they are members of a particular religious sect is once admitted there is no telling where it may end and it will be a subject of infinite vexation and annoyance in the future.

"A BLUFF ON THE PART OF THE JEWS
AND THE STEAMSHIP COMPANIES"
1910

No subject is more important in the history of the Jews in the United States than the subject of immigration. The Jew as an immigrant is the essential story of the Jew in this country. The following document is the full "statement" of a witness, Cyrus L. Sulzberger, before the Committee on Immigration and Naturalization of the House of Representatives at a hearing granted to those opposed to any further restriction of immigration. The presentation is offered in full because it provides insights and arguments which have much relevancy for today's ethnic issues.

STATEMENT OF CYRUS L. SULZBERGER, ESQ., OF NEW YORK
CITY

Before taking up the question generally, I want to call attention to an interesting point in connection with white slavery, with reference to a statement in the Report of the Commissioner-General on page 117, dealing with the subject of white slaves. I desire to point out that, so far as white slavery and its attendant evils come to us by immigration, such immigration is only in very limited degree from Europe, but is chiefly from this continent. The total number of persons debarred from entering because of prostitution or procuring is 504. (Report of Commissioner-General, 1909, pp. 80-81.) Of this number 279 were from Mexico, who sent us 11,000 immigrants over 14 years of age, and 225 were from the rest of the world, which sent us 651,523 immigrants over 14 years of age. (Commissioner-General's Report, p. 22.) Of the 225 coming from Europe who were debarred, the distribution was as follows:

French, 37, or 19 per 10,000 over 14 years.
Scotch, 19, or 13.7 per 10,000 over 14 years.
English, 39, or 11.7 per 10,000 over 14 years.
Irish, 21, or 7.2 per 10,000 over 14 years.
German, 31, or 6.4 per 10,000 over 14 years.
Dutch and Flemish, 4, or 6.3 per 10,000 over 14 years.
Hebrew, 15 or 3.5 per 10,000 over 14 years.
Italian, 22 or 1.3 per 10,000 over 14 years.

It will thus be observed that so far as the European immigration of this undesirable class is concerned, it is greatest among those races classed by the restrictionists as desirable and least among those classed as undesirable. Furthermore, it is observable that the Hebrews and Italians (which of the Europeans have the largest percentage of illiterates) have the smallest percentage of these miscreants, while the French, Scotch, English, Irish, and Germans have a much larger percentage. It is also observable that the amount of money shown (Commissioner-General's Report, p. 23) is least among the Hebrews and Italians and greatest among the others. It would therefore appear that so far as white slavery is concerned, neither the illiteracy of the immigrant nor his lack of funds has any bearing.

I want now to direct your attention to the subject of criminality, and to point out an extraordinary blunder made in the Report of the Commissioner-General of Immigration for the year 1904, in which, on page 59, he gives the total population of the United States as 75,994,575, and the total alien population of the United States as 1,001,595. That is the report of the year 1904, referred to in the current report; the report for the year 1909 (p. 6) refers to the report for the year 1908; the report for the year 1908 refers back to this table from the report of 1904. I find, according to the census report of 1900, volume 1, part 1, page ccix, that of male aliens of voting age there are 1,004,217; that is to say, there are more male aliens of voting age than the total number of aliens given in the Report of the Commissioner-General. In addition thereto there are foreign-born persons of voting age as to whom it is not known whether they are alien or citizen, 748,506. Ignoring entirely all the female aliens of any age, and all the male aliens below voting age, we find that there were more male aliens of voting age than the total number of aliens upon which the whole table of statistics as to criminality and dependency is built, and the use of which in 1904 is repeated in 1908 and 1909. I have made some investigations on my own account upon this subject, and in view of the fact that there are 75 per cent of 748,000 persons of voting age as to whom we do not know whether they are aliens or citizens, but do know that they are foreign born, it has seemed to me that it would be wiser to deal with the question of foreign birth rather than with the question of citizenship, inasmuch as if the man is to become a dependent or a criminal, he is just as apt to become so if he has taken out his citizenship papers as if he has not. I find, then, dealing with foreign born rather than with aliens, in the special reports issued by the Census Bureau (United States Census Report on Prisoners and Juvenile Delinquents in Institutions, 1904), it is said, on page 18:

> If the general population of all ages be taken, the basis for comparison will not be equitable for several reasons. Inmates of the general prisons are all at least 10 years of age and nearly all over 15. For the most part the immigrants are between 15 and 40 years of age. The number of children under 10 years of age is extremely small among the white immigrants as compared with the native whites. In view of these facts, a comparison of the proportions of each nativity class in the white prison population with the corre-

sponding proportions of the general population of all ages would clearly be unfair, for the inclusion of children under 10 years of age would so increase the proportion of natives in the general population that it would seem as if crime were more prevalent among the foreign born as compared with the native white than is actually the case. Therefore, children under 10 years of age are omitted, and the figures given for the population in Table 7 refer only to those at least 10 years of age. Even with this exclusion the figures are, on the whole, less favorable to the foreign-born white prisoners than the facts warrant, as no account could be taken of the large immigration between 1900 and 1904.

And on page 19 this report says:

The figures presented above give little support to the belief that the foreign born contribute to the prison class greatly in excess of their representation in the general population.

In the Census Report on Population, volume 2, pages 112 to 117, it appears that the total foreign-born population, 15 to 19 years of age, is 563, 527. The total foreign-born population being 10, 460, 085, we find that of the foreign-born persons, 5.4 were between 15 and 19 years of age, whereas of the foreign-born persons committed to prison during 1904, 4.6 were from 15 to 19 years of age, showing that there were fewer foreign-born persons from 15 to 19 years of age committed to prison than their percentage in the population.

The Industrial Commission Report, volume 15, part 2, page 287, calls attention to the fact that criminality is 3 to 5 times greater in males than females, and that persons under 20 seldom commit crime. Taking, therefore, male persons 20 years of age and upward, we find that the 1900 census, Population, part 2, pages 112 to 116, that there are 26 per cent foreign-born whites and 74 per cent native-born whites 20 years of age and upward. Turning to the report on prisoners, page 40, we observe that of the major offenders committed during 1904, 21.7 per cent were foreign born and 78.3 per cent native born, notwithstanding the fact that the percentage of foreign-born adult males is 26. That report says, on the same page:

The foreign born do not contribute to the white major offenders above their representation in the general population at least 15 years of age, except in the two Southern divisions, where they are comparatively unimportant. In the Western division, and more especially in the North Central, the proportion of foreign born is considerably lower among the white major offenders than in the white general population.

Among the white minor offenders the proportion of foreign born is generally higher than among the white major offenders, and in the North Atlantic, South Atlantic, and Western divisions, exceeds the proportion of foreign born in the general white population. In the North Central division the foreign born contribute 23.3 per cent of the general white population at least 15 years of age and only 21.3 per cent of the white minor offenders. From these figures, as well as from those for the prisoners enumerated on June 30, 1904, it is evident that the popular belief that the foreign born are filling the prisons has little foundation in fact. It would seem, however, that they are slightly more prone than the native whites to commit minor offenses. Possible to some degree this is attributable to the fact that foreign-born whites are more highly concentrated in urban communities.

Turning to New York State (Census Report, Population, vol. 2, pp. 112-116), we find that the number of native-born males of 20 years of age and upward in New York is 1,362,300; foreign born, 844,563, or 61.7 per cent native born and 38.3 per cent foreign born. In the Special Report on Prisoners, page 18, table 7, we find that of the white prisoners enumerated in New York State on June 30, 1904, 68 per cent were native born and 32 per cent foreign born, the foreign born contributing, therefore, six thirty-eighths, or about 16 per cent less than their ratio in the community, and in view of the fact that 38.3 per cent of the adult male population of New York is foreign born, the statement made by the Superintendent of Prisons and quoted by Mr. Burnett (Hearings, p. 41), as to 25 per cent of the prisoners in Sing Sing, Auburn, and Clinton, is favorable to the foreigners rather than otherwise. It must always be remembered, too, that the census figures are for 1900 and the report on prisoners for 1904, there being no allowance made for the number of foreigners who came into the country in those four years.

Interesting, too, is the following from page 18 of the Special Report on Prisoners:

Even the North Atlantic States, which have absorbed most of the late immigration, show a larger percentage of native prisoners than in 1890. It is evident, therefore, that the huge recent additions of foreigners to the population are not reflected in the prison returns in the degree the prison statistics of 1890 might have led one to expect.

And on pages 19-20:

Certain offenses, especially some comprehended under the general group "against society," are not crimes in the true sense of the word. For instance, no less than 4701 prisoners were sentenced for drunkenness, 2773 for disorderly conduct (which is often only another term for drunkenness), 4287 for vagrancy, and 709 for violating liquor laws, but it does not by any means follow that all these persons, or even a majority of them, should be described as criminals.

There were, in 1890, 28.3 per cent foreign born prisoners and 71.7 per cent native born. Comparing this with the figures for 1904, we find that there were 23.7 per cent foreign born and 76.3 per cent native born, showing a decline of foreign-born prisoners between 1890 and 1904--precisely those years that are coincident with the large immigration of the so-called "undesirable classes."

From page 14, "Report on Prisoners," the following figures are taken:

NUMBER OF PRISONERS PER 100,000 POPULATION
IN 1890 AND 1904

	1890	1904
New York	191	126
Pennsylvania	123	92
Illinois	102	60
Massachusetts	233	187
New Jersey	169	131

These 5 States, which have the largest proportion of immigrants, all show decreases, whereas substantial increases are shown in New Hampshire, Vermont, West Virginia, Florida, Kansas, Wyoming, and Washington, where the immigrant population is small.

In the hearing given by this committee, Mr. Patten, a representative of the Immigration Restriction League, spoke of the fact that 21 per cent of the foreign-born prisoners were unable to read and write. I want to point out that this in itself shows nothing.

Of the native-born prisoners, only 7 per cent were illiterates and 93 per cent were literates, and the argument might be made that literacy causes crime. The fact is that the entire foreign population, as shown by the statistics reported in the volume of prisoners, is less prone to criminality than the native. Instead of its being true, as Mr. Patten says, that "statistics show, as one would expect, that it is the illiterate who generally has criminal propensities," statistics show that of the more than 3,200,000 white illiterates in the whole country the total number of white illiterate prisoners was about 6000. Therefore, to draw any wild inference as to illiteracy generally showing criminal propensities, is a statement not borne out by the facts.

Mr. Patten also says, on page 69, that the literacy test is proposed merely as a means of sifting out the unassimilative elements. What constitute the unassimilative elements does not appear, but if the ability to read and write in the second generation is any test of assimilativeness, it would seem that all the foreign elements assimilate without delay. We find by the census report (Population, part 2, table 10, p. cvi) the following percentage of illiteracy:

	Native whites of native parents	Native whites of foreign parents
United States	5.7	1.6
North Atlantic	1.7	1.5
South Atlantic	12.0	2.1
North Central	2.8	1.3
South Central	11.6	6.8
Western division	3.4	1.3

So that in every separate division the illiteracy is greater among native-born children of native parents than it is among native-born children of foreign parents. It would seem, therefore, that the immigration raises our educational standards instead of degrading them.

On page 50 of the Hearings, Mr. Patten quotes the report of the commissioner at Ellis Island as follows:

Between these elements--

the very bad--

> and those that are a real benefit to the country (as so many of our immigrants are) there lies a class who may be quite able to earn a living here, but who in doing so tend to pull down our standards of living.

These elements are presumably such as the Commissioner-General in his Report speaks of as "economically undesirable," and which under that heading are added to the excluded classes in the Elvins bill. I have seen no definition of what constitutes "an economically undesirable" immigrant, but I assume it to be one who arrives without much money and with a physique that would not qualify him for the United States Army, the test proposed in the Elvins bill, and who is, to a considerable degree, illiterate. If that be the correct description, the average Jewish immigrant would probably fall under that heading. The conditions under which he has lived and from which he is fleeing have restricted his educational possibilities, his physical growth, and his accumulation of wealth. He comes

here with a percentage of illiteracy, a physical development somewhat below our own, and a depleted purse. Large numbers of such Jewish immigrants have arrived in this country since 1880. So far, however, from
pulling down our standards of living, they have done the reverse.

The men's and women's clothing industry is one which is almost exclusively in the hands of these immigrants, both as employers and employees,
and gives us, therefore, an almost perfect illustration of their influence
upon industry and their tendency to reduce or elevate the standard of living.
We find by the Census Report on Manufactures (part 1, 1905, p. ccxxxiv,
table clxix) that while the produce of all industries increased from $11,411,
000,000 in 1900 to $14,802,000,000 in 1905, an increase of 29.7 per cent,
the clothing industry increased from $436,000,000 in 1900 to $604,000,000
in 1905, an increase of 38.5 per cent; in other words, while in 1900 clothing
formed 3.8 per cent of all industries, in 1905 it formed 4.1 per cent of all
industries. Only last month a clothing manufacturer from New York re-
turned from abroad, having established agencies in London, Paris, Berlin,
Vienna, Brussels, and other cities for New-York-made clothing. This is
the second or third manufacturer who has recently put American-made
clothing upon European markets, and in all likelihood a large foreign commerce in manufactured clothing, the product of immigrant labor, will ensue.

Taking the Special Census Reports on Manufactures (part 1, 1905, pp.
164-168) we find that in the production of $604,000,000 worth of clothing
there was paid for wages to men, the sum of $60,943,153, or an average
of $601 per capita against an average earning of men in all industries of
$534 per capita (same vol., p. 22); and to women $46,864,351 or an average
of $317 per capita, as against $298 per capita earned by women in all industries. Inasmuch as the 147,000 women engaged in the clothing industry
are earning 6 per cent more wages than women in all industries, and the
101,000 men engaged in this industry are earning 13 per cent higher wages
than the men in all industries, it would seem in this industry, almost monopolized by immigrant labor, as though immigrant labor were advancing
rather than lowering the standard of living. Furthermore, between the
census of 1880 and the census of 1905, we had the period of high immigration of the so-called "undesirable classes." In 1880 the average wages in
all industries were $344; in 1905 they were $477, an advance of 39 per cent
in the twenty-five years of high immigration.

Much concern is expressed about the cost to the country of maintaining
foreign-born dependents. I do not suppose anybody will charge Mr. Prescott F. Hall, Secretary of the Immigration Restriction League, with being
too friendly to the immigrants. I am going to read you an extract from his
book, "Immigration," commencing on page 67:

> In estimating the money value of the immigrant, attention
> may first be called to the fact that the bulk of our immigra-
> tion is of the age of greatest productiveness; that is to say,
> this country has the benefit of an artificial selection of

adults of working age. For example, in 1903, less than 12 per cent of all immigrants were under 14 years of age; leaving more than 83 per cent between the ages of 14 and 45. In other words, the expense of bringing up the bulk of our immigrants through childhood has been borne by the countries of their birth or residence, and this amount of capital therefore comes to us without expenditure. Professor Mayo-Smith refers to the frequently quoted estimate of Frederick Kapp that the cost of bringing up a child to the age of 15 is $562.50 in Germany and $1000 to $1200 in the United States. Taking the value of the immigrant at $1000, the immigration over 14 years of age in 1903 would have added $754,615,000 to the wealth of the United States if it had all remained in the country. A thoroughly conservative estimate is probably that of Mr. John B. Webber, formerly Commissioner of Immigration at the Port of New York. He assumes that there were 10,000,000 foreign born at the date of the Eleventh Census, and that 2,000,000 of them were working at an average wage of $1 per day; and he points out that these persons added $600,000,000 per year to the earnings of this country.

Taking these figures, we find that the immigration of a single year adds $754,000,000 to the wealth of the country by a saving in the cost of the upbringing of the immigrant, and that the industrial activity of the immigrant adds $600,000,000 annually to the earnings of the country. In view of this statement we need not concern ourselves very much with the fact that a small percentage of immigrants become dependents. That the amount of dependency among immigrants should be larger than among natives is perfectly natural; they are engaged in those occupations in which they are subjected to the risk of physical injury, and being in a strange land when they fall into distress, they lack friends or relatives to care for them.

In view of the fact that the immigrant brings in $750,000,000 as new capital, and adds $600,000,000 annually to the product of the country, it seems to me that what it costs to maintain those in public institutions who may happen to fall into public institutions, becomes negligible.

Another statement that has been made is that of Gen. Francis A. Walker, a statement quoted by Mr. Prescott F. Hall, that the foreign immigration does not add to our population, but that it simply supplants the native population; that when immigrants come in by Ellis Island they do not come in by the natural route. Mr. Hall says in his book, on page 117:

> In many of the older countries of Europe the birth rate has continued with full vigor. In the country from which there has been a considerable emigration, the birth rate immediately increases to such a degree that the pressure of the population is soon restored to its former condition.

As a matter of fact, it is a universal symptom--there is not a single exception--that the birth rate nowhere increases, but almost everywhere decreases. The Encyclopedia of Social Reform, 1908, page 117, gives a comparative statement of the birth rates in the various countries of Europe.

Country	1857-1899	1900	1906[1]
Austria	38.0	....	1903 ⌉
			35.0 ⌋
Belgium	30.1	28.9	1903 ⌉
			27.5 ⌋
Denmark	31.3	29.8	1904 ⌉
			29.2 ⌋
England and Wales	32.3	28.7	1904 ⌉
			28.0 ⌋
France	23.7	21.4	1904 ⌉
			20.9 ⌋
Germany	37.2	35.6	1904 ⌉
			34.1 ⌋
Hungary	42.9	39.3	1903 ⌉
			36.6 ⌋
Ireland	23.8	22.7	1904 ⌉
			23.6 ⌋
Italy	36.6	32.9	1903 ⌉
			31.5 ⌋
Norway	30.7	30.1	1904 ⌉
			27.9 ⌋
Prussia	37.7	36.1	....
Scotland	32.2	29.6	1904 ⌉
			28.6 ⌋
Spain	[2] 35.6	34.4	1902 ⌉
			35.6 ⌋
Sweden	28.7	26.9	1903 ⌉
			25.7 ⌋
United Kingdom	31.1	28.2	....

At the hearing on February 22, Mr. Gardner, of this committee, is quoted as saying:

The greatest experiment in distribution that has been made was that made by the State of South Carolina. They received 762 immigrants from Berlin and Belgium and other places, and the result of that experiment was that, within

---

[1] Statistisches Jahrbuch für das deutsche Reich   [2] 1888-1899.

a year, out of the 762 immigrants all but 72 had disappeared
from the State and had gone elsewhere.

Mr. Prescott F. Hall, in a recent letter, speaks of the distribution as
being a "bluff on the part of the Jews and the steamship companies." Both
Mr. Hall and Mr. Gardner are mistaken. "The greatest experiment in distribution" was not made in the State of North Carolina, but by the Industrial
Removal Office, of New York City, and its work is no bluff. According to
the latest report of this office, there have been sent from New York 45,711
persons, of whom 24,123 were breadwinners, the remainder being their
wives and children. These 24,123 persons represented 221 occupations,
and were sent to 1278 cities and towns, and the 3500 distributed in 1909
were sent to 298 cities and towns. These persons have been distributed to
all parts of the United States, towns and villages as well as cities, and,
according to the records of the office, 85 per cent of the breadwinners are
engaged in gainful occupations at the places to which they were sent. These
persons are distributed through the co-operation of friendly committees in
the receiving places, excepting where the receiving places are small.
Where we send a larger number, we have a reception committee to whom
we send these people, not in response to immediate requisition, but from
a general knowledge of the conditions as to what kind of workingmen they
can use, and we send such classes of workingmen as may be useful in the
particular community. These reception committees consist of public-
spirited citizens of the Jewish community in the locality, who are interested
in the work. They know perfectly well that they are able to place them;
otherwise they would not ask us to send them. If they were to load themselves up with persons for whom no work was procurable, they would have
upon their shoulders the responsibility of caring for those people and making
dependents of them.

In 1909 we sent 3504 breadwinners, of whom 33 went to the New England States, to 11 cities; 401 to the Middle Atlantic States, 78 cities; 254
to the Southern States, 51 cities; 2123 to the Central States, 126 cities;
680 to the Rocky Mountain and Pacific States, to 32 cities; and 13 to Canada,
to 3 cities.

Here are the occupations of the 24,000 who were distributed between
1902 and 1909. They were engaged in 221 occupations; 9.97 per cent in
wood working; 9.17 per cent in metal working, all classified here according to the various branches of metal and wood working; 8.03 per cent in the
building trades; 0.93 per cent in printing and lithography; 20.86 per cent
in the needle industries, clothing, and millinery supplies; 6.99 per cent in
leather; 0.77 per cent in tobacco; 1.95 per cent in miscellaneous trades,
as album makers, bedspring makers, bristle workers, being only a few of
a kind; 1.52 per cent non-manufacturing--barbers, bartenders, bottlers,
canvassers, cleaners, dyers, cooks, domestics, firemen, and so forth;
men without trades, 31.65 per cent, being in numbers 7637. Of that number 7328 were unskilled laborers and 309 were peddlers. 1.75 per cent

farming; 3.36 per cent small dealers in foodstuffs, bakers, brewers, butchers, confectioners, distillers, and so forth, making the number 809, out of 24,000. 3.6 per cent are office help, professional, and so forth.

Of the breadwinners whom we sent away 85 per cent are engaged at the places to which we sent them. Of the remaining 15 per cent some go to other places, about 3 per cent drift back to New York, 12 per cent get to other places and into other occupations, some of these, no doubt, into peddling. I have no knowledge about that, because after we have lost sight of them in the place in which we originally put them, we do not know what has become of them, but we have the records to demonstrate that 85 per cent of them are engaged at the jobs in which we succeeded in getting them occupation.

In response to questions with regard to what steps had been taken to induce immigrants to engage in farming, Mr. Sulzberger made the following statement with regard to the work of the Jewish Agricultural and Industrial Aid Society: That society engages in placing Jews upon farms. I do not like to adduce figures without having the figures before me, so I will not mention figures at all. The abandoned farms of New England the Jews have made to flourish once more, and we have farmers in pretty nearly every State in the United States. We began a year ago the publication of the "Yiddish Farmer" (a farm journal in the Yiddish language), which, although it is only a year old, has a paid subscription list that many older established papers would be glad to have. The Jewish farmer is in every respect able to hold his own along with any other, and is showing a very strong tendency and desire to get to the farm.

In addition to this society there is one in Chicago, the Jewish Agriculturists' Aid Society, which does similar work.

A farm school, of which Rev. Dr. Joseph Krauskopf, of Philadelphia, is President, is conducted at Doylestown, Pa., where trained agriculturists are turned out, and the Baron de Hirsch Fund has a similar school in Woodbine, N.J., where they are conducting a similar work. The Government has taken from that school a large number of experts for its agricultural service all over the country. There is a greater tendency toward farming on the part of the Jewish people than since its dispersion.

As respects congestion, our experience in New York is that, whereas a few years ago we had one Jewish quarter, we now have many. The Jews who come from Russia have a natural tendency to live together, because they wish to live where their language is spoken. But they do not all live in one part of the city by any means. We have a large Jewish settlement on the lower East Side, we have a large Jewish settlement in Harlem, we have a large Jewish settlement in the Bronx, and several large Jewish settlements in Brooklyn. I believe that the amount of congestion on the lower East Side of New York is to-day less than it was eight or ten years ago, because of this spreading. The same thing is true about the Italians. They have spread over various settlements, instead of being concentrated in one. I want to call attention to a matter, in connection with congestion, that is generally overlooked: While in the large cities there is always a state of more or less congestion, the persons involved are not the same persons. In other words, a man who comes to the City of New York and settles down on the lower East Side stays there three or four or five years. After the lapse of a few years he moves on and comes up into the Harlem settlement. From there he goes to the Bronx, and presently he is on Fifth Avenue.

The greatness of the City of New York has been brought about by its immigrant population. If we had no immigrant population in New York, perhaps it might be better upon some sides, but it might be worse upon others. That is a large question to decide. Hundreds of thousands of men have made New York their home. When I arrived in New York, I had what was left out of $25, after paying my railroad fare from Philadelphia to New York. I have succeeded in making good to a reasonable extent. Hundreds of thousands have come from Europe who have made good in the same way, and it would have been a fatal blunder to have sent all these men off on the farms or to other parts, when they were fitted to work out and have worked out their salvation and economic success, and have done it right there in the City of New York. I appreciate the difficulties and dangers of congestion. I do not suppose that any man appreciates them any more than I, because I have spent a great deal of time in the study of that matter, but we must not get hysterical about it, because those men who have gathered there have made that city great, and are making it greater day by day. It is the greatest city in the country to-day, and in a short time it will be the greatest city in the world. If you say to the immigrant population that it must go there no more, but must scatter through various parts of the United States, it would be good for the various parts of the United States, but it would be bad for New York.

As respects the Americanization of the immigrants, it proceeds at the most wonderful rate. So far as their reading foreign newspapers is concerned, it does not seem to me that that at all interferes with their Americanization. A man's thought may be thoroughly sympathetic with our American thought, and yet he may express it in another language. I do not know why a man who reads a German newspaper or an Italian newspaper or a Yiddish newspaper should not think along American lines as well as if he expresses himself in the English language.

As to an educational test, I will add that if we had not the laborer, irrespective of his ability to read, we would find great difficulty about getting our heavy work done, in view of the great demand for labor in this country to-day. From my observation of the matter I am convinced that with all the immigrants we have we are not to-day responsive to the demand for labor. As I have said before, illiteracy and crime have no connection, and the fact that a man is illiterate should not weigh either for or against him in considering admitting him to the country. There may be reasons for debarring him, but illiteracy is not one of them, because there does not seem to be anyone I can find anywhere who says there is a connection between illiteracy and crime.

"THE RIGHTEOUS INDIGNATION ENTERTAINED
BY JEWS EVERYWHERE TOWARD ME"
1927

In 1920 Henry Ford took on the anti-Semitic, forged document, "The Protocols of the Elders of Zion" and distributed
it through his company's publication, the Dearborn Independent. These "protocols" charged that there was a plot
to establish a world-wide Jewish dictatorship. In 1927, following a libel suit, Ford published the following retraction
and apology.

For some time I have given consideration to the series of articles concerning Jews which since 1920 have appeared in the Dearborn Independent.
Some of them have been reprinted in pamphlet form under the title The International Jew. Although both publications are my property, it goes without saying that in the multitude of activities it has been impossible for me
to devote personal attention to their management or to keep informed as to
the contents. It has therefore inevitably followed that the conduct and pol-
icies of these publications had to be delegated to men whom I placed in
charge of them and upon whom I relied implicitly.

To my great regret I have learned that Jews generally and particularly
those of this country not only resent these publications as promoting anti-
Semitism, but regard me as their enemy. Trusted friends with whom I have
conferred recently have assured me in all sincerity that in their opinion
the character of the charges and insinuations made against the Jews, both
individually and collectively, contained in many of the articles which have
been circulated periodically in the Dearborn Independent and have been reprinted in the pamphlets mentioned, justifies the righteous indignation en-
tertained by Jews everywhere toward me because of the mental anguish oc-
casioned by the unprovoked reflections made upon them.

This has led me to direct my personal attention to this subject, in order
to ascertain the exact nature of these articles. As a result of this survey
I confess that I am deeply mortified that this journal, which is intended to
be constructive and not destructive, has been made the medium for resur-
recting exploded fictions, for giving currency to the so-called Protocols of
the Wise Men of Zion, which have been demonstrated, as I learn, to be
gross forgeries, and for contending that the Jews have been engaged in a
conspiracy to control the capital and the industries of the world, besides
laying at their door many offenses against decency, public order, and good
morals.

Had I appreciated even the general nature, to say nothing of the details,
of these utterances, I would have forbidden their circulation without a moment's hesitation, because I am fully aware of the virtues of the Jewish

people as a whole, of what they and their ancestors have done for civilization and for mankind toward the development of commerce and industry, their sobriety and diligence, their benevolence, and their unselfish interest in the public welfare.

Of course there are black sheep in every flock, as there are among men of all races, creeds, and nationalities who are at times evildoers. It is wrong, however, to judge a people by a few individuals, and I therefore join in condemning unreservedly all wholesale denunciations and attacks.

Those who know me can bear witness that it is not in my nature to inflict insult upon and to occasion pain to anybody, and that it has been my effort to free myself from prejudice. Because of that I frankly confess that I have been greatly shocked as a result of my study and examination of the files of the Dearborn Independent and of the pamphlets entitled The International Jew.

I deem it my duty as an honorable man to make amends for the wrong done to the Jews as fellow men and brothers, by asking their forgiveness for the harm I have unintentionally committed, by retracting so far as lies within my power the offensive charges laid at their door by these publications, and by giving them the unqualified assurance that henceforth they may look to me for friendship and goodwill.

Finally, let me add that this statement is made on my own initiative and wholly in the interest of right and justice and in accordance with what I regard as my solemn duty as a man and as a citizen.

APPENDIX I.

Estimated American Jewish Population by State

State	Estimated Jewish Population	Total Population	Estimated Jewish % of Total
Alabama	9,465	3,558,000	0.27
Alaska	190	274,000	0.07
Arizona	20,485	1,663,000	1.23
Arkansas	3,065	1,986,000	0.15
California	693,085	19,300,000	3.59
Colorado	25,140	2,043,000	1.23
Connecticut	103,730	2,963,000	3.50
Delaware	8,540	534,000	1.60
D.C.	15,000	809,000	1.85
Florida	189,280	6,151,000	3.08
Georgia	26,310	4,568,000	0.58
Hawaii	1,000	780,000	0.13
Idaho	500	703,000	0.07
Illinois	283,180	10,991,000	2.58
Indiana	24,385	5,061,000	0.48
Iowa	7,500	2,774,000	0.27
Kansas	3,515	2,293,000	0.15
Kentucky	11,200	3,220,000	0.35
Louisiana	15,630	3,726,000	0.42
Maine	8,185	976,000	0.84
Maryland	177,115	3,754,000	4.72
Massachusetts	259,635	5,469,000	4.75
Michigan	97,995	8,739,000	1.12
Minnesota	33,565	3,647,000	0.92

State	Estimated Jewish Population	Total Population	Estimated Jewish % of Total
Mississippi	4,015	2,344,000	0.17
Missouri	80,685	4,625,000	1.74
Montana	615	693,000	0.09
Nebraska	8,100	1,439,000	0.56
Nevada	2,380	449,000	0.53
New Hampshire	4,260	702,000	0.61
New Jersey	387,220	7,093,000	5.46
New Mexico	3,645	1,006,000	0.36
New York	2,521,755	18,078,000	13.95
North Carolina	9,450		
Ohio	160,715	10,588,000	1.52
Oklahoma	6,480	2,520,000	0.26
Oregon	9,045	2,008,000	0.45
Pennsylvania	443,595	11,728,000	3.78
Rhode Island	23,000	914,000	2.52
South Carolina	7,285	2,664,000	0.27
South Dakota	520	656,000	0.08
Tennessee	16,710	3,975,000	0.42
Texas	65,520	10,977,000	0.60
Utah	1,650	1,034,000	0.16
Vermont	2,330	425,000	0.55
Virginia	37,350	4,595,000	0.81
Washington	15,485	3,276,000	0.47

State	Estimated Jewish Population	Total Population	Estimated Jewish % of Total
West Virginia	4,760	1,802,000	0.26
Wisconsin	32,295	4,225,000	0.77
Wyoming	710	315,000	0.23
Total U.S.	5,868,555	199,861,000	2.94

(Source: U.S. Bureau of the Census, Current Population Reports, Population Estimates, Series P-25, No. 420, 1969)

Jewish Population Estimates, with permission, American Jewish Yearbook 1970, Vol. 71, American Jewish Committee, New York.

APPENDIX II.

Selected and Annotated Bibliography

Antin, Mary. The Promised Land. Boston: Houghton Mifflin,
    1969.
    An autobiographical account describing the journey
    of the Jews from Russia to America.

Baron, Salo W., and Blau, Joseph L., editors. A Documentary
    History of the Jews of the United States: 1790-1840.
    3 vols. Philadelphia: Jewish Publication Society:
    New York; Columbia University Press, 1964.
    Evidence of Jewish involvement in American life
    during the early years of the Republic.

Glazer, Nathan. American Judaism. Chicago: University of
    Chicago Press, 1957 (Paperback)
    A socio-historical analysis of the American Jewish
    community and its roots in Europe.

Grinstein, H.B. Rise of the Jewish Community of New York.
    Philadelphia: Jewish Publication Society, 1945.
    A scholarly account of Jewish history in New York.

Handlin, Oscar. Adventure in Freedom: 300 Years of Jewish
    Life in America. New York: McGraw-Hill, 1954.
    A leading historian's interpretation of American
    Jewish history through 1954.

Hapgood, H. The Spirit of the Ghetto: Studies of the Jewish
    Quarter of New York. New York: Schocken, 1965
    (Paperback)
    A Perceptive and charming account of the turn of the
    century Jewish community in New York. A contemp-
    orary account. Beautiful drawings by Jacob Epstein.

Janowsky, Oscar I., editor. The American Jew: A Reappraisal.
    Philadelphia: Jewish Publication Society, 1964.
    Essays describing the features of the American
    Jewish community and its institutions.

Korn, Bertram W. American Jewry and the Civil War. New
    York: Harper & Row; Philadelphia: Jewish Publicat-
    ion Society, 1962.
    The Jewish role, on both sides, in the Civil War.

Ketzer, Morris N. Today's American Jew. New York: McGraw-
    Hill, 1967.
    The current Jewish scene dealing with social,
    cultural, political, religious, and educational
    elements in American Jewish life.

Levinger, Lee Joseph. A History of the Jews in the United States. New York: Union of American Hebrew Congregations, revised edition. 1970.
A textbook history for junior high children.

Lebeson, Anita L. Pilgrim People. New York: Harper & Bros., 1950.
An older, out of print, study. But it remains one of the best histories of American Jewry.

Levitan, Tina. The Jew in American Life. New York: Hebrew Publishing Company, 1969.
Short but compelling biographies of notable Jews in American history from colonial period through the present period.

Rubinger, Naphtali. Abraham Lincoln and the Jews. New York: Jonathan David, 1962.
A comprehensive account of a phase of the struggle for Jewish rights and the background and makeup of 19th Century American Jewry.

Teller, Judd L. Strangers and Natives: The Evolution of the American Jew From 1921 to the Present. New York: Delacorte Press, 1968.
A study of the immigrant American Jew.

Rischin, Moses. The Promised City, New York's Jews, 1870-1914. New York: Citadel Press, 1964. (Paperback)
The mass migration of the Eastern Jews and their mutual interaction with their new environment in America.

Useful Out of Print Studies for Research Purposes

Frank, Waldo. The Jew in Our Day. New York: Duell, Sloan & Pearce, 1944.

Freund, Miriam K. Jewish Merchants in Colonial America. New York: Behrman House Inc., 1939.

Friedman, Lee M. Early American Jews. Cambridge: Harvard University Press, 1934.

Friedman, Lee M. Jewish Pioneers and Patriots. Philadelphia: Jewish Publication Society, 1942.

Friedman, Theodore and Gordis, Robert. editors, Jewish Life in America. New York: Horizon Press, 1955.

Goodman, Abram V. American Overture. Philadelphia: Jewish Publication Society, 1947.

Joseph, Samuel. History of the Baron De Hirsch Fund. The
        Americanization of the Jewish Immigrant. Phila-
        delphia: Jewish Publication Society, 1935.

Learsi, Rufus. The Jews in America. A History. New York:
        World Publishing Co., 1954

Levine, Louis. The Women's Garment Workers. A History of
        the International Ladies' Garment Workers' Union.
        New York: Huebsch, 1924.

Levitan, Tina. The Firsts of American Jewish History. New
        York: Charuth Press, 1952.

Marcus, Jacob R. Early American Jewry: The Jews of New
        York, New England and Canada, 1649-1794.
        Philadelphia: Jewish Publication Society, 1951.

Marcus Jacob R. Early American Jewry: The Jews of Pennsyl-
        vania and the South, 1655-1790. Philadelphia:
        Jewish Publication Society, 1953.

Marcus, Jacob R. Memoirs of American Jews. Philadelphia:
        Jewish Publication Society, 1955-56.

Mersand, Joseph. Traditions in American Literature. A Study
        of Jewish Characters and Authors. New York:
        Modern Chapbooks, 1939.

Pool, David De Sola. Portraits Etched in Stone: Early
        American Settlers. New York: Columbia University
        Press, 1952.

Schappes, Morris U. A Documentary Story of the Jews in the
        United States. New York: Citadel Press, 1950.

Wiernik, Peter. History of the Jews in America. New York:
        Jewish History Publishing Company, 1931.

APPENDIX III.

AUDIO-VISUAL MATERIALS ON AMERICAN JEWISH LIFE AND

HISTORY

Films:

The American Jew
(45 minutes. Sponsored and distributed by Anti-Defamation
League. Nominal rental fee; inquire at ADL regional offices)
Portrays the story of the Jews in the U.S. and their contributions
to American civilization.

American Morning
(15 minutes. Free rental. Distributed by Union of American Hebrew
Congregations)
Depicts the role of the Union of American Hebrew Congregations
and Hebrew Union College in shaping Liberal Judaism and their
contribution to the life and culture of the American Jewish community.

Between Two Eternities
(30 minutes. Rental $8.50. Distributed by the National Academy
for Adult Jewish Studies of the United Synagogue of America)
Depicts episodes in the life of Solomon Schecter, teacher, scholar
and one of the architects of Conservative Judaism in the U.S.

The Gift
(30 minutes. Rental $8.50. Distributed by the National Academy
for Adult Jewish Studies of the United Synagogue of America)
Incidents in the life of Judah Touro. Highlights Touro's liberation
of his slave, and points up the true meaning of the gift of freedom.

The Golden Years
(14 minutes. Sale and rental prices on request. Prints provided for
single showings by communal, educational, and religious groups
without charge. Sponsored and distributed by Federation of Jewish
Philanthropies of New York)
Portrays the rehabilitation of a 63-year old jobless tailor at a
workshop vocational center, operated for ages handicapped men
and women by an employment and guidance agency affiliated with
the Federation of Jewish Philanthropies of New York.

Lawyer From Boston
(30 minutes. Rental $8.50. Distributed by the National Academy for
Adult Jewish Studies of the United Synagogue of America.)
Highlights episodes in the life of Louis D. Brandeis, and tells how
he discovered his Jewish heritage.

The Pugnacious Sailing Master
(30 minutes. Rental $8.50. Distributed by the National Academy for
Adult Jewish Studies of the United Synagogue of America)
Tells the story of Uriah P. Levy, who was instrumental in the abolition of corporal punishment in the United States Navy. It vividly
depicts the anti-Semitism to which he was subjected, and his re-
luctance to conceal his Jewish identity.

A Small Triumph
(28 minutes. Rental $10.00; special educational rate $3.00. Sponsored and distributed by National Council of Jewish Women)
Describes a community service project of the National Council of
Jewish Women. It shows how, through the efforts of dedicated
volunteers, blind children are integrated into classes with sighted
children in Cincinnati public schools.

To Be As One
(31 minutes. Rental $15.00. Distributed by Jewish Center Lecture
Bureau, National Jewish Welfare Board)
Aims to portray the Jewish Community Center program by focusing
its story on the activities of a typical Jewish Center.

Young Sam Gompers
(30 minutes. Rental $8.50. Distributed by the National Academy
for Adult Jewish Studies of the United Synagogue of America)
Shows the early life of Samuel Gompers, whose participation in the
labor movement culminated in the founding of the American Federation of Labor.

Filmstrips:

The Jews in America
(2 parts. Sale $7.50 each. Produced and distributed by the Jewish
Education Committee of New York. Includes accompanying scripts)
Part I covers the years between 1654 and 1860. Memorable highlights are depicted, including the arrival of the first Jews in America, their role in the Revolutionary War, and the westward movement to California. Part II spans the last hundred years, showing
Jewish participation in the Civil War, the cause and effect of the
influx of East Europeans, the development of American Jewish culture, and the growth of social, religious, and communal activities
in the American Jewish community.

Albert Einstein
(Sale $7.50, including accompanying script. Produced and distrib-
uted by Jewish Education Committee of New York)
Einstein's life story depicted against the events of his time.

American Jewry in the Civil War
(Sale $7.50. Produced and distributed by Jewish Education Committ-
ee of New York)

Beginning with ante-bellum days, this filmstrip covers the social, religious and fraternal life of American Jewry. It highlights their efforts to organize synagogues, philanthropic and relief organizations, and the roles they played in the Civil War.

Haym Salomon-Financier of the Revolution
(Sale $7.50. Distributed by the Union of American Hebrew Congregations)
An account of the life of Haym Salomon, showing his patriotic endeavors towards the cause of liberty, as well as his financial aid during the American Revolution.

Isaac Mayer Wise: Master Builder of American Judaism
(Sale $7.50, including teacher's guide. Produced and distributed by the Commission on Jewish Education, Union of American Hebrew Congregations)
Tells the dramatic story of an important dynamic religious leader. It describes his adventures, his struggles and his ultimate success in creating the major institutions of Reform Judaism in this country.

Judah Touro-Friend of Man
(Sale $7.50, including teacher's guide. Record of narration is also available $2.00. Distributed by Commission on Jewish Education, Union of American Hebrew Congregations)
Illustrates the story of the life and work of Judah Touro, the American Jewish patriot and philanthropist, and the growth of the American Jewish community in which he played an important part.

Major Noah
(Sale $7.50, including teacher's guide. Produced and distributed by Jewish Education Committee of New York)
Describes the colorful life of Mordecai Manuel Noah-adventurer, journalist, U.S. consul, editor, and dreamer of a Jewish State in Ararat, the island in the Niagra River.

Rabbi Stephen S. Wise: A Twentieth Century Prophet
(Sale $7.50, including teacher's guide. Record $2.00. Sponsored and distributed by the Commission on Jewish Education, Union of American Hebrew Congregations)
A review of the life of Rabbi Wise, highlighting his leadership in the religious, Zionist and cultural affairs of the American Jewish community, as well as the role he played in combatting prevailing social evils.

300 Years: Memorable Events in American Jewish History
(Sale $7.50; record $2.50. Distributed by the Commission on Jewish Education, Union of American Hebrew Congregations)
Traces the participation of the Jews in the westward movement and in the various explorations which extended the frontiers of the United States, and lays stress on the developement of the American Jewish community and its religious institutions.

Through the Years: Jewish Women in American History
(Sale $7.50, including script. Sponsored and distributed by The
National Federation of Temple Sisterhoods)
Deals with the contributions of Jewish women to the life of the
Jewish and the general community in America for the past three
centuries.

APPENDIX IV.

American Jewish Civic Organizations

Civic	Founded	Location
American Council for Judaism	1943	NYC*
American Jewish Committee	1906	NYC
American Jewish Conference on Soviet Jewry	1964	NYC
American Jewish Congress	1917	NYC
American Jewish Congress: Women's Division	1933	NYC
Anti-Defamation League	1913	NYC
Association of Jewish Community Relations Workers	1950	NYC
Bureau for Careers in Jewish Service	1968	NYC
Commission on Social Action of Reform Judaism	1953	NYC
Conference of Presidents of Major American Jewish Organizations	1955	NYC
Consultative Council of Jewish Organizations	1946	NYC
Coordinating Board of Jewish Organizations	1947	Washington D.C.
Council of Jewish Organizations in Civil Service	1948	NYC
Jewish Labor Committee	1933	NYC
Jewish Labor Committee: Women's Division	1947	NYC
Jewish Labor Committee: Workmen's Circle	1940	NYC
Jewish War Veterans of the United States of America	1896	Washington D.C.
National Association of Jewish Center Workers	1965	NYC

*New York City

Civic	Founded	Location.
National Jewish Commission on Law and Public Affairs	1965	NYC
National Jewish Community Relations Advisory Council	1966	NYC
North American Jewish Youth Council	1966	NYC
World Jewish Congress	1936	NYC

Social & Cultural

Alexander Kohut Memorial Foundation	1915	NYC
American Academy for Jewish Research	1920	NYC
American Biblical Encyclopedia Society	1930	NYC
American Histadrut Cultural Society	1964	NYC
American Jewish Historical Society	1892	Waltham, Mass.
American Jewish Institute	1947	NYC
American Jewish Information Bureau	1932	NYC
American Jewish Press Association	1943	Fort Worth, Texas
Association of Jewish Libraries	1966	Camden, N.J.
Central Yiddish Culture Organization	1938	NYC
Conference on Jewish Social Studies	1933	NYC
Congress for Jewish Culture	1948	NYC
Hebrew Arts School for Music and Dance	1952	NYC

Social & Cultural	Founded	Location
Hebrew Culture Foundation	1955	NYC
Histadruth Ivrith of America	1916	NYC
Jewish Academy of Arts and Society	1927	Philadel- phia
Jewish Book Council of America	1940	NYC
Jewish Liturgical Music Society of America	1936	NYC
Jewish Museum	1904	NYC
Jewish Publication Society of America	1888	Philadelphia
Leo Baeck Institute	1954	NYC
Louis and Esther LeMed Fund	1939	Silvercrest, Mich.
Memorial Foundation for Jewish Culture	1964	NYC
National Foundation for Jewish Culture	1960	NYC
National Hebrew Culture Council	1952	NYC
Union of Russian Jews	1942	NYC
Yiddisher Kultur Farband	1937	NYC
Yivo Institute for Jewish Research	1925	NYC

Overseas Assistance		
American Committee of OSE	1940	NYC
American Council for Judaism Philanthropic Fund	1955	NYC
American Friends of the Alliance Israelite Universelle	1946	NYC
American Jewish Joint Distribution Committee-JDC	1914	NYC

Overseas Assistance	Founded	Location
American ORT Federation- Organization for Rehabilitation Through Training	1924	NYC
A.R.I.F.-Association Pour Le Retablissement des Institutions et Oeuvres Israelitetes en France	1944	NYC
Conference on Jewish Materials Claims Against Germany	1951	NYC
Freeland League for Jewish Territorial Colonization	1938	NYC
Jewish Restitution Successor Organization	1948	NYC
United HIAS Service	1884	NYC
United Jewish Appeal	1939	NYC
United Jewish Appeal: Women's Division	1946	NYC
Vaad Hatzla Rehabilitation Committee	1939	NYC
Women's Social Service for Israel	1937	NYC

Religious and Intellectual		
Academy for Jewish Religion	1954	NYC
Agudas Israel World Organization	1912	NYC
Agudath Israel of America	1912	NYC
American Association for Jewish Education	1939	NYC
Association of Jewish Chaplains of the Armed Forces	1946	NYC
Association of Orthodox Jewish Scientists	1947	NYC
B'nai B'rith Hillel Foundations	1923	Washington D.C.

Religious and Intellectual	Founded	Location
B'nai B'rith Youth Organization	1924	Washington D.C.
Brandeis Institute	1941	Brandeis, Calif.
Cantors Assembly	1947	NYC
Central Conference of American Rabbis	1889	NYC
Central Yeshivah Beth Joseph Rabbinical Assembly	1941	Brooklyn, N.Y.
College of Jewish Studies	1925	Chicago, Ill.
Commission on Status of Jewish War Orphans of Europe, American Section	1945	NYC
Dropsie University	1907	Philadelphia
Federation of Jewish Student Organizations	1937	NYC
Gratz College	1895	Philadelphia
Hebrew College	1921	Brookline, Mass.
Hebrew Theological College	1922	Skokie, Ill.
Hebrew Union College; Jewish Institute of Religion of Cincinnati, New York, and Los Angeles	1875, 1922 merged 1950; 1954	Cincinnati NYC Los Angeles
Herzliah Hebrew Teachers Institute and Jewish Teachers Seminary and People's University	1967	NYC
Jewish Chautauqua Society	1893	NYC
Jewish Ministers Cantors Association	1940	NYC
Jewish Teachers Association-Morim	1926	NYC

Religious and Intellectual	Founded	Location
Jewish Theological Seminary of America	1886; 1902	NYC
League for Safeguarding the Fixity of the Sabbath	1929	NYC
Mesivta Yeshiva Rabbi Chaim Berlin Rabbinical Academy	1905	Brooklyn, N.Y.
Mirrer Yeshiva Central Institute	1947	Brooklyn, N.Y.
National Association of Hillel Directors	1949	St. Louis, Mo.
National Bar Mitzvah Club	1962	NYC
National Committee for Furtherance of Jewish Education	1926	NYC
National Council for Jewish Education	1926	NYC
National Council for Torah Education of Mizrachi-Hapoel Hamizrachi (Religious Zionists of America)	1939	NYC
National Council of Young Israel	1912	NYC
National Federation of Hebrew Teachers and Principals	1944	NYC
National Jewish Information Service for the propogation of Judaism	1960	Los Angeles, Calif.
Ner Israek Rabbinical College	1933	Baltimore, Md.
Ozar Hatorah	1946	NYC
P'eylim-American Yeshiva Student Union	1951	NYC
Rabbinical Alliance of America (Igud Harabbanim)	1944	NYC
Rabbinical Assembly	1900	NYC
Rabbinical College of Telshe	1941	Wickliffe, Ohio

Religious and Intellectual	Founded	Location
Rabbinical Council of America	1923	NYC
Research Institute of Religious Jewry	1941	NYC
Sholem Aleichem Folk Institute	1918	NYC
Society of Friends of the Touro Synagogue National Historic Shrine	1948	Newport, R.I.
Synagogue Council of America	1924	NYC
Torah Umesorah-National Society for Hebrew Day Schools	1944	NYC
Union of American Hebrew Associations	1873	NYC
Union of Orthodox Jewish Congregations of America	1898	NYC
Union of Orthodox Rabbis of the United States and Canada	1902	NYC
Union of Sephardic Congregations	1929	NYC
United Lubavitcher Yeshivoth	1940	Brooklyn, N.Y.
United Synagogue of America	1913	NYC
West Coast Talmudical Seminary	1953	Los Angeles, Calif.
World Union for Progressive Judaism	1926	NYC
Yavne Hebrew Theological Seminary	1924	Brooklyn, N.Y.
Yavneh National Religious Jewish Students Association	1960	NYC
Yeshiva University	1886	NYC
Yeshivath Chachmey Lublin	1942	Detroit, Mich.
Yeshivath Torah Vodaath and Mesivta Rabbinical Seminary	1918	Brooklyn, N.Y.

Fraternal	Founded	Location
American Federation of Jews From Central Europe	1942	NYC
American Veterans of Israel	1949	NYC
Association of Yugoslav Jews in the United States	1940	NYC
Bnai Zion-The American Fraternal Zionist Organization	1908	NYC
Brith Abraham	1887	NYC
Brith Sholom	1905	Philadelphia
Central Sephardic Jewish Community of America	1940	NYC
Farband-Labor Zionist Order	1913	NYC
Free Sons of Israel	1849	NYC
International Jewish Labor Bund	1897	NYC
Jewish Peace Fellowship	1941	NYC
Jewish Socialist Verband of America	1921	NYC
Mu Sigma Fraternity	1906	NYC
Progressive Order of the West	1896	St. Louis, Mo.
Sephardic Jewish Brotherhood of America	1915	Bronx, N.Y.
United Order of True Sisters	1846	NYC
United Rumanian Jews of America	1909	NYC
Workmen's Circle	1900	NYC
World Sephardic Federation	1951	NYC

Welfare	Founded	Location
American Jewish Correctional Chaplains Association	1937	NYC
American Jewish Society for Service	1950	NYC
American Medical Center at Denver	1904	Spivak, Colo.
Baron de Hirsch Fund	1891	NYC
B'nai B'rith	1843	Washington, D.C.
City of Hope	1913	Los Angeles, Calif.
Council of Jewish Federations and Welfare Funds	1932	NYC
Deborah Hospital	1922	Brown Mills, N.J.
Hope Center for the Retarded	1965	Denver, Colo.
International Council on Jewish Social and Welfare Services	1961	NYC
Jewish Agricultural Society	1900	NYC
Jewish Braille Institute of America	1931	NYC
Jewish Conciliation Board of America	1920	NYC
Jewish National Home for Asthmatic Children	1907	Denver, Colo.
Jewish Occupational Council	1939	NYC
Leadership Conference of National Jewish Women's Organization	1925	NYC
Leo N. Levi Memorial National Arthritis Hospital	1914	Hot Springs, Ark.
National Association of Jewish Family, Children's, and Health Services	1965	Worcester, Mass.

Welfare	Founded	Location
National Conference of Jewish Communal Service	1899	NYC
National Council of Jewish Women	1893	NYC
National Jewish Committee on Scouting	1926	New Brunswick, N.J.
National Jewish Hospital and Research Center at Denver	1899	Denver, Colo.
National Jewish Welfare Board	1917	NYC
World Federation of YMHAs and Jewish Community Centers	1947	NYC

Israel-Related		
America-Israel Cultural Foundation	1939	NYC
American Committee for Boys Town of Jerusalem	1949	NYC
American Committee for the Weizmann Institute of Science	1944	NYC
American Friends of the Hebrew University	1931	NYC
American Friends of the Tel Aviv University	1955	NYC
American Friends of Religious Freedom in Israel	1963	Massapequa, N.Y.
American Israel Public Affairs Committee	1954	Washington, D.C.
American-Israeli Lighthouse	1928	NYC
American Jewish League for Israel	1957	NYC
American Physicians Fellowship for the Israel Medical Association	1950	Brookline, Mass.
American Red Mogen Dovid for Israel	1941	NYC

Israel-Related	Founded	Location
American Society for Technion-Israel Institute of Technology	1940	NYC
American Zionist Youth Foundation	1963	NYC
Americans for a Music Library in Israel	1950	Chicago, Ill.
Ampal-American Israel Corporation	1942	NYC
Bar-Ilan University in Israel	1952	NYC
Brit-Trumpeldor, Inc. Betar	1935	NYC
Dror Young Zionist Organization	1948	NYC
Federated Council of Israel Institutions	1940	NYC
Haddassah-The Women's Zionist Organization of America	1912	NYC
Hagdud Haivri League	1929	NYC
Hashomer Hatzair	1950	NYC
Hatzaad Harishon	1964	NYC
Hebrew University-Technion Joint Maintenance Appeal	1954	NYC
Theodor Herzl Foundation	1954	NYC
Israel Music Foundation	1948	NYC
Jewish Agency-American Section	1929	NYC
Jewish National Fund, Inc.	1910	NYC
Keren-Or (Jerusalem Institutions for the Blind)	1958	NYC
Mizrachi Women's Organization of America	1925	NYC
National Committee for Labor Israel	1923	NYC
National Young Judea	1909	NYC
PEC Israel Economic Corporation	1926	NYC

Israel-Related	Founded	Location
Palestine Symphonic Choir Project	1938	NYC
Poale Agudath Israel of America	1948	NYC
Poale-Zion-United Labor Zionist Organization of America	1905	NYC
Rassco Israel Corporation	1950	NYC
Religious Zionists of America	1934	NYC
Society of Israel Philatelists	1948	Woodside, N.Y.
State of Israel Bond Organization	1951	NYC
United Charity Institutions of Jerusalem	1903	NYC
United Israel Appeal	1927	NYC
United States Committee-Sports for Israel	1948	NYC
Women's League for Israel	1928	NYC
World Confederation of General Zionists	1946	NYC
Zebulun Israel Seafaring Society	1946	NYC
Zionist Organization of America	1897	NYC

APPENDIX V.

American Jewish Newspapers & Periodicals by State

Alabama

Birmingham. Jewish Monitor, monthly

Arizona

Phoenix. Phoenix Jewish News, bi-weekly
Tuscon. Arizona Post, bi-weekly

California

Los Angeles. B'nai B'rith Messenger, weekly
California Jewish Voice, weekly
Heritage-Southwest Jewish Press, weekly
Jewish Community Directory, annual
Los Angeles Reporter, weekly
San Francisco. California Jewish Record, bi-weekly
Jewish Star, irregular
San Francisco Jewish Bulletin, weekly

Colorado

Denver. Intermountain Jewish News, weekly

Connecticut

Hartford. Connecticut Jewish Ledger, weekly

Delaware

Wilmington. Jewish Voice, bi-weekly

District of Columbia (Washington)

American Jewish Journal, quarterly
Jewish Heritage, quarterly
Jewish Veteran, monthly
Jewish Week, weekly
National Jewish Monthly, monthly

Florida

Jacksonville. Southern Jewish Weekly, weekly
Miami. Jewish Floridian, weekly
West Palm Beach. Our Voice, monthly

Georgia

Atlanta. Southern Israelite, weekly

Illinois

    Chicago. Chicago Jewish Post and Opinion, weekly
            Jewish Information, irregular
            Jewish Way-Unzer Weg, quarterly
            Sentinel, weekly
            The Torch, quarterly

Indiana

    Indianapolis. Indiana Jewish Post and Opinion, weekly
              Indiana Jewish Chronicle, weekly

Kentucky

    Louisville. Kentucky Jewish Post and Opinion, weekly

Louisiana

    New Orleans. The Jewish Civic Press, weekly

Maryland

    Baltimore. Baltimore Jewish Times, weekly

Massachusetts

    Boston. Jewish Advocate, weekly
    Brookline. Jewish Times, weekly
    Springfield. Jewish Weekly News, weekly
    Waltham. American Jewish Historical Quarterly, quarterly

Michigan

    Detroit. The Jewish News, weekly.

Minnesota

    Minneapolis. American Jewish World, weekly
    White Bear Lake. St. Paul Jewish News, bi-weekly

Missouri

    Kansas City. Kansas City Jewish Chronicle, weekly
    St. Louis. Missouri Jewish Post, weekly
           St. Louis Jewish Light, bi-weekly

Nebraska

    Omaha. Jewish Press, weekly

Nevada

Las Vegas. Las Vegas Israelite, weekly

New Jersey

Atlantic City. Jewish Record, weekly
Highland Park. Jewish Journal, semi-monthly
Jersey City, Jewish Standard, weekly
Marlton Pike, Voice, bi-weekly
Newark, Jewish News, weekly

New York

Buffalo. Buffalo Jewish Review, weekly

New York City. Adult Jewish Education, irregular
American Examiner, weekly
American-Israel Economic Horizons, bi-
monthly
American Jewish Yearbook, annual
American Zionist, monthly
Aufbau, weekly
Bitzaron, monthly
B'nai Yiddish, bi-monthly
CCAR Journal, quarterly
Central Conference of American Rabbis
Yearbook, annual
Commentary, monthly
Congress Bi-Weekly, bi-weekly
Conservative Judaism, quarterly
Day-Jewish Journal, daily
Dimensions in American Judaism, bi-monthly
Education in Judaism, bi-monthly
Farband News, bi-monthly
Freeland, irregular
Freie Arbeiter Stimme, monthly
Haddassah Magazine, monthly
Hadoar Hebrew Weekly, weekly
Hadorom, bi-annual
Hapardes, monthly
Histadrut Foto-News, 7 times a year
Ideas, quarterly
In Jewish Bookland, 7 times a year
U Institutional and Indutrial Kosher
Products Directory, annual
Israel Horizons, monthly
Israel Magazine, monthly
Jewish Audio-Visual Review, annual
Jewish Book Annual, annual
Jewish Braille Review, monthly
Jewish Collegiate Observer, quarterly

New York.   Jewish Current Events, bi-weekly
(cont.)   Jewish Daily Forward, daily
            Jewish Education, quarterly
            JEC Bulletin, irregular
            Jewish Education Newsletter, quarterly
            Jewish Education Register and
                Directory, quinquennial
            Jewish Frontier, monthly
            Jewish Homemaker, bi-monthly
            Jewish Horizon, quarterly
            Jewish Life, bi-monthly
            Jewish Music Notes, semi-annually
            Jewish Observer, monthly
            Jewish Parent, quarterly
            Jewish Post and Opinion, weekly
            Jewish Press, weekly
            Jewish Social Studies, quarterly
            Jewish Spectator, monthly
            Jewish Telegraphic Agency Community
                News Reporter, weekly
            Jewish Telegraphic Agency News
                Digest, weekly
            Jewish Youth Monthly, monthly
            Journal of Jewish Communal Service,
                                        quarterly
            Judaism, quarterly
            Keeping Posted, 15 times a year
            Kinder Journal, bi-monthly
            Kinder Zeitung, bi-monthly
            U Kosher Products Directory, annual
            Kultur un Lebin-Culture and
                Life, bi-monthly
            Midstream, monthly
            Der Mizrachi Weg, bi-monthly
            Mizrachi Woman, monthly
            Morning Freiheit, daily
            National Census of Jewish
                Schools-Information Bulletin, Treinnial
            News of the Yivo-Yedies Fun
                Yivo , quarterly
            U News Reporter, irregular
            Olomeinu-Our World, monthly
            Or Hamizrach, quarterly
            Our Age (Dorenu), bi-monthly
            Oyen Shvel, bi-monthly
            U Passover Products Directory, annual
            Pedagogic Reporter, quarterly
            Perspectives, irregular
            Pioneer Woman, monthly
            Proceedings of the American Academy
                for Jewish Research, annual

New York.   Proceedings of the Rabbinical
(cont.)   Assembly, annual
    Rabbinical Council Record, bi-monthly
    Reconstructionist, tri-weekly
    Response, quarterly
    Sheviley Hachinuch, quarterly
    Shmuessen Mit Kinder Un Yugent, monthly
    Synagogue Light, bi-monthly
    Synagogue School, quarterly
    Synagogue Service, quarterly
    Talks and Tales, monthly
    Technion, bi-monthly
    Tradition, quarterly
    Undzer Aygn Vinkl, quarterly
    United Synagogue Review, quarterly
    Unser Tsait, monthly
    Der Wecker, monthly
    Women's League Outlook, quarterly
    Workmen's Circle Call, bi-monthly
    World Over, bi-monthly
    Yavneh, Review, annual
    Yavneh Studies, bi-monthly
    Di Yiddishe Heim, quarterly
    Yiddishe Kultur, monthly
    Dos Yiddishe Vort, monthly
    Yiddisher Kemper, monthly
    Yiddishe Shrakh, 3 times a year
    Yivo Annual of Jewish Social
      Science, irregular
    Yivo Bleter, irregular
    Young Israel Viewpoint, monthly
    Young Judean, monthly
    Youth and Nation, bi-monthly
    Zukunft, monthly

Rochester. Jewish Ledger, weekly

Schenectady. Jewish World, weekly

North Carolina

    Greensboro. American Jewish Times-Outlook, monthly

Ohio

    Canton. The Stark Jewish News, monthly
    Cincinnati. American Israelite, weekly
        American Jewish Archives, semi-annual
        Hebrew Union College Annual, annual
        Studies in Bibliography and
          Folklore, bi-annual

Cleveland. <u>Cleveland Jewish News</u>, weekly
Columbus. <u>Ohio Jewish Chronicle</u>, weekly
Dayton. <u>Dayton Jewish Chronicle</u>, weekly
Toledo. <u>Toledo Jewish News</u>, monthly
Youngstown. <u>Youngstown Jewish Times</u>, bi-weekly

Oklahoma

Oklahoma City. <u>Southwest Jewish Chronicle</u>, quarterly
Tulsa. <u>Tulsa Jewish Review</u>, monthly

Pennsylvania

Pittsburgh. <u>Jewish Chronicle</u>, weekly
Philadelphia. <u>Jewish Exponent</u>, weekly
              <u>Jewish Leader</u>, monthly
              <u>JPS Bookmart</u>, quarterly
              <u>Jewish Quarterly Review</u>, quarterly
              <u>Philadelphia Jewish Times</u>, weekly
              <u>Torch</u>, quarterly

Rhode Island

Pawtucket. <u>Rhode Island Herald</u>, weekly
Providence, <u>Rhode Island Jewish Historical</u>
                     <u>Notes</u>, irregular
Tennessee

Memphis. <u>Hebrew Watchman</u>, weekly
Nashville. <u>Observer</u>, weekly

Texas

Dallas. <u>Texas Jewish Post</u>, weekly
Houston. <u>Jewish Digest</u>, monthly
          <u>Jewish Herald-Voice</u>, weekly

Washington

Seattle. <u>Jewish Transcript</u>, bi-weekly

Wisconsin

Milwaukee. <u>Wisconsin Jewish Chronicle</u>, weekly